Gvantsa Davitashvili, Thomas Kruessmann, and
Ivanna Machitidze (eds.)

The 'New' Geopolitics in the Caucasus

What Role for the EU?

EUROPEAN STUDIES IN THE CAUCASUS

Edited by Thomas Kruessmann

1   *Andrey Makarychev and Thomas Kruessmann (eds.)*
     Europe in the Caucasus, Caucasus in Europe
     Perspectives on the Construction of a Region
     ISBN 978-3-8382-1328-6

2   *Oliver Reisner, Selin Türkeş-Kılıç, Gaga Gabrichidze (eds.)*
     Experiencing Europeanization in the Black Sea and South Caucasus
     Inter-Regionalism, Norm Diffusion, Legal Approximation and Contestation
     ISBN 978-3-8382-1458-0

3   *Thomas Kruessmann (ed.)*
     The Caucasus in Europe-Asia Connectivity
     The Promise of Infrastructure and Trade
     ISBN 978-3-8382-1574-7

4   *Gvantsa Davitashvili, Thomas Kruessmann, and Ivanna Machitidze (eds.)*
     The 'New' Geopolitics in the Caucasus and the EU's Role
     ISBN 978-3-8382-1707-9

Gvantsa Davitashvili, Thomas Kruessmann,
and Ivanna Machitidze (eds.)

THE 'NEW' GEOPOLITICS IN THE CAUCASUS
What Role for the EU?

Bibliografische Information der Deutschen Nationalbibliothek
Die Deutsche Nationalbibliothek verzeichnet diese Publikation in der Deutschen Nationalbibliografie; detaillierte bibliografische Daten sind im Internet über http://dnb.d-nb.de abrufbar.

Bibliographic information published by the Deutsche Nationalbibliothek
Die Deutsche Nationalbibliothek lists this publication in the Deutsche Nationalbibliografie; detailed bibliographic data are available in the Internet at http://dnb.d-nb.de.

Disclaimer: "The European Commission's support for the production of this publication does not constitute an endorsement of the contents, which reflect the views only of the authors, and the Commission cannot be held responsible for any use which may be made of the information contained therein."

Cover picture: ID 27124674 © Hugoht | Dreamstime.com

ISBN-13: 978-3-8382-1707-9
© *ibidem*-Verlag, Hannover • Stuttgart 2024
Alle Rechte vorbehalten

Das Werk einschließlich aller seiner Teile ist urheberrechtlich geschützt. Jede Verwertung außerhalb der engen Grenzen des Urheberrechtsgesetzes ist ohne Zustimmung des Verlages unzulässig und strafbar. Dies gilt insbesondere für Vervielfältigungen, Übersetzungen, Mikroverfilmungen und elektronische Speicherformen sowie die Einspeicherung und Verarbeitung in elektronischen Systemen.

All rights reserved. No part of this publication may be reproduced, stored in or introduced into a retrieval system, or transmitted, in any form, or by any means (electronic, mechanical, photocopying, recording or otherwise) without the prior written permission of the publisher. Any person who commits any unauthorized act in relation to this publication may be liable to criminal prosecution and civil claims for damages.

Printed in the EU

Table of Contents

Thomas Kruessmann
Foreword 7

Gvantsa Davitashvili, Thomas Kruessmann, and Ivanna Machitidze
Introduction 9

Giorgi Beridze
Biopolitics and Europeanization: Change and Continuity of Foreign Policy Discourses in the South Caucasus 19

Diana R. Galoyan and Albert A. Hayrapetyan
EU-Armenia Relations as a Test Case for International Relations Theories 47

Ruben Elamiryan and Archil Sikharulidze
Colored versus Velvet: Revolutions in Georgia and Armenia 77

Anahit Babayan
Challenges of European Integration: The Cases of Armenia and Georgia 99

Ashot Aleksanyan
Hybrid War against European Political Integration of Armenia: A Dead End or a Springboard on the Way to the EU? 123

Nino Jibuti
The EU in Nagorno-Karabakh: Irreversible Rapprochement or Elusive Partnership? 145

Bios 169

Foreword

Dear reader!

The volume at hand is the final deliverable of the Jean Monnet Support to Associations grant which AESC held until mid-2022. And again, this work of collaborative writing has had a complicated history. Originally planned to be an outcome of the 2022 Convention in Baku, the event was cancelled in a move that precipitated the conflicts between Armenia and Azerbaijan over Nagorno-Karabakh. It also served as a signal that European Studies, especially with a focus on the "new" geopolitics in the region, were not currently welcome in Azerbaijan. Thankfully, many committed scholars stayed the course and prepared manuscripts. A year later, however, when the next Convention was scheduled for Yerevan, the ethnic Armenian population had just fled Nagorno-Karabakh and Armenia proper, including scholars and universities, were grappling with the consequences. So, unfortunately, the 2023 Convention had to be cancelled as well.

Another reason for regret is that for several years now the EU, under the Erasmus+ Programme, has stopped to offer Jean Monnet funding to associations. Available funding flows directly to universities and higher education ministries for structural change. But the problem is that Ph.D. students are often left alone in how to bridge the gap between elaborating a Ph.D. thesis and establishing an internationally visible publication record. It is here where AESC remains to have its ongoing mission, however, in an increasingly difficult environment.

Maneuvering all these difficulties and producing not only a hardcopy, but also an open access version of the book is in no small part the achievement of ibidem Press. I would like to use this opportunity to thank Mr. Christian Schön and his dedicated team of professionals for their patience and unwavering support. Let us hope that the result will reach a large audience of interested readers in the Caucasus and beyond. As we devote much attention to young scholars, this volume is also meant to be a practical encouragement to continue with publishing and to strive towards peer-reviewed international journals.

Per aspera ad astra!

Thomas Kruessmann,
Series Editor,
AESC President

Introduction

Gvantsa Davitashvili, Thomas Kruessmann, and Ivanna Machitidze

Ever since the demise of the USSR, small states in the South Caucasus have been experiencing vulnerability due to a variety of domestic and external factors. Recent hopes to leave the shadow of great power competition and embrace multipolarity have been shattered when Russia engaged in its full-scale invasion of Ukraine. In general, small states have fewer options to pursue when it comes to promoting their vital national interests. A series of recent studies discusses strategies for small states to adapt to "multipolarity without multilateralism" and disillusionment with the normative and rules-based arrangements guaranteeing their security (Lebanidze and Kakachia 2023; Mihalski et al. 2024, Dobrescu 2023).

Neo-realist paradigm argues that bandwagoning or sheltering is the most likely option for a small state to undertake. This strategy emphasizes the need for a security umbrella of a stronger state which nevertheless may compromise the autonomy of foreign policy decision-making (Gvalia et al. 2013; Vaicekauskaite 2017). Another option is hedging, distancing from long-term obligations in the framework of the regional cooperation arrangements to maneuver between large regional powers or alliances (Kuik 2021). Neutrality, unlike hedging, avoids membership in regional political-military blocs, but with the same goal of preserving autonomous decision-making in a crucial security realm. This approach, until the eventual joining of NATO, was pursued by Sweden and Finland (Michalski 2024).

While the "labels" for each state in the South Caucasus have seemed unchangeable over time, the second Nagorno-Karabakh war in 2020 and Russia's full-scale invasion of Ukraine provoked geopolitical shifts of a scale unseen before. Whereas Georgia, previously addressed as the poster child of democratic transformation, has been experiencing the erosion of fragile democratic institutions and its government embarking on Eurosceptic rhetoric, Armenia openly criticized its long-term security provider Russia, a development hard to imagine a decade ago. With no support to prevent its territorial losses to Azerbaijan, Armenia has been eager to invest in cooperation with the EU, but is still a long way from obtaining candidate status (Çakmak, Özsahin 2023; Atanesyan et al. 2023). Azerbaijan has been the most consistent in its long-term foreign policy strategy so far, maneuvering the West and Russia to achieve its key security goals, namely the restoration of its territorial integrity and retaking Nagorno Karabakh under its de facto control (Valiyev and Mamishova 2019). Apart from the role of Türkiye which is openly supporting Azerbaijan, it is "the Russian factor" which is behind most developments.

Whereas two decades ago the EU had been perceived as an outsider, its role in the South Caucasus evolved from enhancing good governance and democratic institutions building alongside the US to contributing to crisis mediation efforts (Börzel et al. 2009). There is now increased geopolitical ambition to play "the-acceptable-party-for-all" card in bringing lasting peace to the region, thereby potentially challenging the dominant role of Russia and Türkiye. Through different frameworks of cooperation, the EU approaches its neighborhood and provides external governance as a projection of its internal policies (Lavenex 2004). Expanding the EU market and guaranteeing security and peace throughout the continent serve as a strong incentive and anchor for unstable regimes (Mény 2023). While geopolitical influences compel the EU to hasten the accession of candidate countries, which is crucial to uphold the credibility of the membership perspective as a driver of domestic reforms, candidates, both present and future, have yet to attain the EU's standards of rule of law (Börzel 2023). As far as the external dimension of Europeanization through policy transfer (Howell 2002) is concerned, Schimmelfennig argues that even non-candidate countries could be analyzed in the context of Europeanization (Schimmelfennig, 2015).

The repertoire of theories responding to these developments has become ever more sophisticated. It is now commonly accepted that Europeanization is not a straightforward and linear process, but a multidirectional, conflictive and ambivalent development that includes ruptures, backlashes and even Eurosceptic reactions (Worschech 2018). Nevertheless, this approach falls short from occupying a dominant position among theoretical viewpoints aiming to grasp the regional shifts in the South Caucasus. Its countries are still commonly seen as the "in-betweens",—the ones in the European "rimland" (Spykman) caught between two conflicting geopolitical views, the one of the West and Russia. There recently has been a tendency to go beyond the approaches as a "traditional zone of privileged interest" (German 2022) when discussing challenge of Russia's hegemony stemming from China, being "in the shadow" of Russia (Skalamera 2022), through "Russian world" (*russkii mir*) concept (Suslov 2018; Pieper 2020), biopolitics (Makarychev and Yatsyk 2017) and the use of hybrid strategies, especially disinformation campaigns and the whipping-up of identity conflicts. There are now "outside-in" (Ademmer, Delcour and Wolczuk 2016; Bouris and Papadimitriou 2020; Delcour and Wolczuk 2021) and "inside-out" perspectives (Dembińska and Smith 2021) that dig into the sub-state level and try to paint a more nuanced picture of the views held by political elites, business interests and civil society. Even classical geopolitics is now subscribing to a 'bottom-up' approach which views geopolitics as "not a sole preserve of states and governments" (Dodds 2019, 5) but involving local communities and ordinary citizens. For instance, Gerard Toal defines the region as a "geopolitical field" comprising "both the sociospatial context of statecraft and the social players, rules, and spatial dynamics constituting the arena" (Toal 2017, 9).

Geopolitics "from below" has become an important research paradigm (Zhurzhenko 2024), extending even to popular geopolitics in cultural studies. Critical geopolitics attempts to deconstruct the clash between territorial power and ideas of spatiality "structured around economic hub and flow imaginaries" (Moisio 2018). While classical geopolitics emphasizes the rootedness of foreign policy decisions in a country's geographic location, critical geography follows a postmodernist approach by highlighting the representation and discourses of geography by various actors such as states, political elites, civil society, public opinion etc. All in all, over the past 30 years critical geopolitics has developed into a broad stream of critical perspectives interested in the spatiality of world affairs, the making of identities and the use of borders (Kuus 2017). The most recent approach, anthropocene geopolitics, goes even further by challenging the set-in-stone character of geographic location by shedding light on how the ecosystems have been challenged due to climate change (Proedrou 2020). This view further stresses the EU's role in leading its member-states to initiate a common approach to security and foreign policy decisions taking into account climate change as key and permanent security challenge.

The variety of theoretical approaches, their interaction, combination and interplay are of critical importance for grasping the multifaceted character of the "EU's geopolitical awakening" and its geopolitical actorness in the South Caucasus and beyond (Raik et al. 2024). Both are visible through the EU's determination to resolving political deadlock and polarization in Georgia, the intensified relations with struggling Armenia, a hybrid regime, and authoritarian Azerbaijan. In this manner, the EU goes beyond the "value dimension only approach" and turns pragmatic, as in the case of keeping the dialogue with Baku in light of its importance for the connectivity strategy and despite the systematic character of human rights violations. In contrast to lumping together post-Soviet countries under the caption of "in-betweens", Sami Moisio argues in favor of a small states perspective peculiar to the South Caucasus (Moisio 2022). His plea to take small states seriously does not only contradict the perspective that the territorial sovereignty of small states "is nothing but a constantly negotiated and contested phenomenon as great powers dominate the international system and engage in security competition with each other" (Moiso 2022), but also a call "towards providing fresh and badly needed perspectives to the violent geopolitical condition as it unfolds today" (Moisio 2022).

Hence, giving voice to both young researchers and seasoned academics from the region is a reflection of the process of self-assertion, of making sense of the often tumultuous and unpredictable events and developing agency in contributing to the future of their countries. Unlike a special issue which would be more tightly woven around a central theme, the chapters provided in this book were suggested by the authors themselves in response to the book's main title. They show a strong desire to take stock of the events and to develop comparative perspectives, primarily between Georgia and Armenia. Needless to say, even after editorial efforts the opinions expressed are exclusively those of the authors.

In the first chapter, *Beridze* takes up the biopolitics paradigm. He offers a critical look at how the debates about the foreign policy priorities of Georgia, Armenia and Azerbaijan are couched in biopolitical discourses about survival and security. He shows how the use of biopolitical discourse has become a means for local leaders to consolidate their power. The next chapter by *Galoyan and Hayrapetyan* is even more strongly theory-driven. The authors use the case of EU-Armenia relations to identify the inherent limitations in the major theories on international relations (IR), to develop an "interparadigm dialogue" by comparing and contrasting the relevant IR theories, and finally to reflect on EU external action policies through the application of the relevant IR theories. Their conclusion is that for the given case study liberal intergovernmentalism in combination with the EU external governance theory offer the best understanding. The following chapter is a discussion of the terms "color revolution" vs. "velvet revolution" as shorthands for the transformations that occurred in Georgia and Armenia. In doing so, *Elamiryan and Sikharulidze* develop a more conceptual framework on what distinguishes the two types of events. They show that, despite being located in the same region and facing the consequences of ethno-political conflicts, Georgia and Armenia took rather different paths in their foreign and security policy making. In the next chapter, *Babayan* continues the comparison on Armenia and Georgia, but using an "outside-in" perspective on how the EU responds to the challenges posed by both countries. Her main finding is that despite the EU's efforts to play an active role in the region, better public participation, awareness-raising, comprehensive knowledge and understanding of the EU in Armenia and Georgia, particularly among civil society organizations, are needed for reaching a success. Embarking on the case of Armenia, *Aleksanyan* shows how the national elites are facing significant domestic opposition in making crucial U-turn decisions on the country's foreign policy course in response to the regional blocks and institutional arrangements that fail to serve the country's key national interests as protection of its sovereignty and territorial integrity. The author traces the path Armenia underwent from the Velvet Revolution till the present, turning from one of Russia's most loyal allies to challenging the viability of Russia-led regional integration blocks such as the Eurasian Economic Union and Collective Security Treaty Organization. The last chapter is devoted to the EU's role in Nagorno-Karabakh. Using critical discourse theory, *Jibuti* examines the statements issued by the EU's respective institutions since 2020, in particular the use of language. Her main question is how and in which regard has the OSCE Minsk Group been ineffective in terms of mediating and reaching sustainable peace since the Second Karabakh war and leading up to the dissolution of the enclave. By scrutinizing the EU-led discourse and its increasingly robust and assertive engagement in the region since the Second Karabakh War, she asks whether deploying unarmed civilian observers to Armenia might imply that the EU is replacing Russia as a mediator in the conflict.

At the time of preparing this volume for publication, geopolitical uncertainty in the region and beyond has been persisting. Due to the events unfolding at an unprecedented pace in the South Caucasus and its neighborhood, the key challenge for scholars is to avoid the role of mere observers catching up with the past. "Outside-in" or "inside-out", "bottom-up" or "top-down", cross-border or international, there is not a single approach to uncover the patterns of behavior, both in terms of regional, state, or sub-state perspectives, where local actors strive to assert agency amid broader power struggles. As each of the chapters above shows, by engaging in dialogue, applying and respecting multi-, inter-, transdisciplinary approaches, and embracing diverse perspectives, all stakeholders can work towards building a more secure and prosperous future for the region.

Bibliography

Ademmer, Esther, Laure Delcour and Kataryna Wolczuk. 2016. "Beyond Geopolitics: Exploring the Impact of the EU and Russia in the 'Contested Neighborhood'." *Eurasian Geography and Economics* 57 (1): 1–18.

Atanesyan, Arthur, Bradley Reynolds and Artur E. Mkrtichyan (2023) "Balancing between Russia and the West: The Hard Security Choice of Armenia." *European Security*, published online doi: 10.1080/09662839.2023.2258528.

Bouris, Dimitris and Dimitris Papadimitriou. 2020. "The EU and Contested Statehood in its Near Abroad: Europeanisation, Actorness and Statebuilding." *Geopolitics* 25 (2): 273-293.

Börzel, Tanja, Yasemin Pamukasemin and Andreas Stahn. 2009. "Democracy or Stability? EU and US Engagement in the Southern Caucasus." In *Promoting Democracy and the Rule of Law*, edited by Amichai Magen, Thomas Risse and Michael A. McFaul, 150–184. London: Palgrave Macmillan.

Börzel, Tanja. 2023. Widening without Deepening: Why Treaty Reforms Will Not Make the EU Fit for Enlargement, *SIEPS:* (2): 54-69: available at: https://www.sieps.se/globalassets/publikationer/2023/sieps-2023_2op-eng-webb.pdf#page=15.

Casier, Tom. 2022. "Why Did Russia and the EU Clash Over Ukraine in 2014, But Not Over Armenia?" *Europe-Asia Studies*, 74(9): 1676-1699.

Çakmak, Cenap and M. Cüneyt Özşahin. 2023. "Explaining Russia's Inertia in the Azerbaijan–Armenia Dispute: Reward and Punishment in an Asymmetric Alliance." *Europe-Asia Studies*, 7(6): 972-988.

Delcour, Laure and Kataryna Wolczuk. 2021. "Mind the Gap: Role Expectations and Perceived Performance of the EU in the South Caucasus." *Eurasian Geography and Economics* 62 (2): 156-177.

Dembińska, Magdalena and David Smith. 2021. "Navigating in-between the EU and Russia." *Eurasian Geography and Economics* 62 (3): 247-263.

Dobrescu, Magdalina. 2023. "Explaining Third-country Participation in CSDP Missions: The Case of the Association Trio—Ukraine, Georgia and Moldova." *European Security* 32(4): 539-557.

Dodds, Klaus. 2019. *Geopolitics. A Very Short Introduction*. Oxford: Oxford University Press.

German, Tracey. 2022. "Russia and the South Caucasus: The China Challenge." *Europe-Asia Studies* 74(9): 1596-1615, DOI: 10.1080/09668136.2022.2071843

Gvalia, Giorgi, David Siroky, Bidzina Lebanidze, and Zurab Iashvili. 2013. "Thinking Outside the Bloc: Explaining the Foreign Policies of Small States." *Security Studies*, published online https://doi.org/10.1080/09636412.2013.757463.

Howell, Kerry. 2002. *Developing Conceptualizations of Europeanization and European Integration: Mixing Methodologies*, Sheffield, UK, available at: https://aei.pitt.edu/1720/1/Howell.pdf.

Kuik, Chen-Chwee. 2021. "Getting Hedging Right: A Small-State Perspective." *Chinese Strategic Review*, published online https://link.springer.com/article/10.1007/s42533-021-00089-5.

Kuus, Merje. 2017. "Critical Geopolitics." *International Studies*, published online https://doi.org/10.1093/acrefore/9780190846626.013.137.

Lavenex, Sandra. 2004. "EU External Governance in 'Wider Europe'." *Journal of European Public Policy*, 11 (4): 680-700.

Lebanidze, Bidzina and Kornely Kakachia. 2023. "Bandwagoning by Stealth? Explaining Georgia's Appeasement Policy on Russia." *European Security* 32(4): 676-695.

Makarychev, Andrey and Alexandra Yatsyk. 2017. "Biopower and Geopolitics as Russia's Neighborhood Strategies: Reconnecting People or Reaggregating Lands?" *Nationalities Papers* 45 (1): 25–40.

Mearsheimer, John J. 2014. "Why the Ukraine Crisis Is the West's Fault: The Liberal Delusions That Provoked Putin." *Foreign Affairs* 93 (5): 77-84 and 85-89.

Mihalski, Anna, Douglas Brommesson and Ann-Marie Ekengren. 2024. "Small States and the Dilemma of Geopolitics: Role Change in Finland and Sweden." *International Affairs* 100 (1): 139–157.

Moisio, Sami. 2018. *Geopolitics of the Knowledge-based Economy*. London: Routledge.

Moisio, Sami. 2022. "Geopolitics of Explaining Russia's Invasion of Ukraine and the Challenge of Small States." *Political Geography* 97.

Pieper, Moritz. 2020. "*Russkiy Mir*: The Geopolitics of Russian Compatriots Abroad." *Geopolitics* 25 (3): 756-779.

Proedrou, Filippos. 2020. "Anthropocene Geopolitics and Foreign Policy: Exploring the Link in the EU Case." *Alternatives: Global, Local, Political*, published online doi:10.1177/0304375420931706.

Raik, Kristi, Steven Blockmans, Anna Osypchuk and Anton Suslov. 2024. "EU Policy towards Ukraine: Entering Geopolitical Competition over European Order." *The International Spectator* 59 (1): 39-58.

Schimmelfennig, Frank. 2015. Europeanization beyond the Member States, *ETH Zurich*, available at: https://www.research-collection.ethz.ch/bitstream/handle/20.500.11850/107421/2/lreg-2015-1.pdf.

Skalamera, Morena. 2022. "Stepping' Out of Russia's Shadow: Russia's Changing 'Energy Power' in Post-Soviet Eurasia." *Europe-Asia Studies*, 74:9, 1640-1656.

Suslov, Mikhail. 2018. "'Russian World Concept': Post-Soviet Political Ideology and the Logic of 'Spheres of Influence'." *Geopolitics* 23 (2): 330-353.

Toal, Gerard. 2017. *Near Abroad: Putin, the West and the Contest over Ukraine and the Caucasus*. Oxford: Oxford University Press.

Tsuladze, Lia, Nino Abzianidze, Mariam Amashukeli, and Lela Javakhishvili. 2023. "De-Europeanization as Discursive Disengagement: Has Georgia "Got Lost" on its Way to European Integration? *Journal of European Integration*, published online DOI: 10.1080/07036337.2023.2278072.

Vaicekauskaite, Zivile. 2017. "Security Strategies of Small States in A Changing World." *Journal on Baltic Security* 3(2): 7-15.

Valiyev, Anar and Narmina Mamishova. 2019. "Azerbaijan's Foreign Policy Towards Russia since Independence: Compromise Achieved." *Southeast European and Black Sea Studies* 19(2): 269-291.

Worschech, Susann. 2018. The 'Making' of Europe in the Peripheries: Europeanization through Conflicts and Ambivalences." *Culture, Practice & Europeanization* 3 (3): 56–76.

Zhurzhenko, Tatiana. 2024. "Everyday Europeanization and Bottom-Up Geopolitics at the Ukrainian-Polish Border." *Geopolitics*, published online https://doi.org/10.1080/14650045.2023.2283488.

Biopolitics and Europeanization: Change and Continuity of Foreign Policy Discourses in the South Caucasus

Giorgi Beridze

Abstract

The South Caucasus is at the beginning of the fourth decade of bloody inner regional conflicts, which also coincides with the decades of independence of the South Caucasian countries. In addition to ethnic and interstate violence, the language used by ruling elites to communicate with society has taken on special significance. In particular, by analyzing the speeches of the leaders of the three countries, I will describe how the discourse about the countries' foreign policy priorities is summarized in well-rehearsed biopolitical discourses about survival and security. The goal of this article is to highlight the use of biopolitical discourse in the context of foreign policy challenges as a means for local leaders to consolidate their power.

Keywords: Biopolitics; Azerbaijan; Armenia; Georgia; Europeanization; Zoepolitics.

Introduction

The South Caucasus region is one of the zones of conflict between the West and Russia. Thirty years of ethnic conflicts and the Russian military presence in the region pose a constant threat to security. All three states in the region take special care of their security responsibilities, which are an integral part of their national interests. Recently, Russia's hegemony in the region has been challenged. Türkiye's conciliation with Azerbaijan, Georgia's European perspective, and Armenia's reform course after the Velvet Revolution can serve as indicators of Russia's decline in the region.

However, the endless nature of existing conflicts poses a constant threat to security and survival in the region. This article analyzes the discourses of the ruling elites in the South Caucasus in the context of the region's conflicts and what outcomes these discourses produce.

In the past decade, all three countries in the region have experienced post-war political stability and increased consolidation of ruling elites (Georgia in 2008, Azerbaijan and Armenia in 2018 and 2020). The remarkable economic growth in Azerbaijan and regime change in Armenia (2018) and Georgia (2012) have greatly encouraged the leaders of these countries to seek new ways of consolidating their legitimacy and gain popular support. It is important to consider that all three ruling elites have successfully emerged from power struggles with their political opponents. Three main elections have been held in Georgia since 2018, where, against the tides of polarization, the "Georgian Dream" (GD) still triumphs and, for the first time in the history of Georgia, leads the country for the consecutive third term. In Armenia, after the 2020 war with Azerbaijan, Nikol Pashinyan's team was able to win early parliamentary elections in 2021, thus strengthening public support. Azerbaijan's triumph in the Nagorno-Karabakh conflict in 2020 makes Ilham Aliyev's dominance in Azerbaijani politics even more substantial.

The current Georgian government has been in power since the October 2012 parliamentary elections, and Georgia's uncompromising stance toward Russia has been fundamentally changed. Georgian authorities refer to this stance as a "policy of normalization of relations with Russia." For example, during the 2012 election campaign, the GD presented a foreign policy vision with the wording "Georgia should not be a point of antagonism between the West and Russia." (Netgazeti 2012).

Moreover, since December 2012, Georgia and Russia have introduced the "dialogue format" in which special delegates, Zurab Abashidze of Georgia and Grigoriy Karasin of Russia, regularly discuss problematic and critical issues arising in and near Georgia's occupied territories. Remarkably, this is the only diplomatic format involving Georgia and Russia.

As a result, Georgian wine and other products immediately entered the Russian market. With the easing of pressure, a new security scenario was created in Georgia. GD demonstrates that the "success" of Georgia's peace strategy with Russia is due to the efforts of the Georgian government. The "success"[i] of GD is based primarily on avoiding the losses and injuries that could be caused by a bloody war of occupation and conquest by the Russian Federation. This discourse has grown considerably since the beginning of the Russian invasion of Ukraine in February 2022. GD has called the opposition a "war party," pointing out potential dangers and using anti-war rhetoric to bolster its credibility.

The Nagorno-Karabakh conflict and the risks it poses are central to the security narratives developed by ruling elites in Azerbaijan and Armenia.[ii] The persecution of Azerbaijanis in the Nagorno-Karabakh region in the early 1990s, as well as the evacuation of a substantial portion of the Armenian population from the province during the 2020 war, are at the root of these issues.

The 2020 Nagorno-Karabakh war modified these narratives cosmetically but qualitatively left them unchanged. The safety of Armenians residing in the retained lands of Nagorno-Karabakh, especially the capital Stepanakert, has become a priority for Armenia's ruling elite. The ruling elites of Azerbaijan underlined the need of preserving the "liberated regions", recalling how tens of thousands of Azerbaijanis were internally displaced or were direct victims of ethnic cleansing conducted by Armenians.

If we return to the idea that the states of the region are still in the process of institutional formation and in many cases of border demarcation (Sammut 2008), although they are finding ways to conduct their own security discourses, we should also note that the discussion of large regional formats (most importantly, of the 3+3 format or the Eastern Partnership, EaP) is one of the central issues in the foreign policy of these states. For the past three decades, the leading elites of Azerbaijan and Armenia have been preoccupied with the prospect of permanent conflict. In fact, both countries are in a state of extreme readiness for war. As a result, social relations are constantly saturated with biopolitical content, and terms such as "survival", "danger" and "sacrifice" help governmental bodies to introduce a biopolitical agenda into their relationship with the society.

The concepts of "war", "survival" and "danger" are often used in Georgia, although their connotations change over time. The postwar period from 2008 to 2012 was characterized by the government referring to the threat from Russia to strengthen the ruling United National Movement (UNM). In addition, the UNM-led administration primarily focused on strengthening the armed forces, establishing spy networks in separatist regions, and voicing anti-Russian narratives.

After the 2012 elections, the new government abandoned this approach. GD constantly warns of the dangers of war. By emphasizing the concepts of survival and security, it focused on diplomatic efforts to prevent danger and portrayed its government as a peacekeeper. Maintaining stable relations with Russia is a fundamental aspect of GD to achieve its biopolitical goal of consolidating power which is partly a denial of rapprochement with Russia as a "threat".

To sum up, the existing security discourses are practically intertwined with the notion of "mortal threat" which the elites of all three countries actively manipulate. It is worth noting that their positioning in relation to major regional formats (for instance, 3+3 or EaP) is directly linked to the concepts of threats and survival.

The Eurasian Economic Union (EAEU) and the 3+3 model are regional projects initiated by non-democratic regimes (Iran, Türkiye, Russia), and the three small countries of the South Caucasus approach these projects cautiously due to security risks. It should be noted that only Georgia has rejected this project outright. At the same time, the existing living threats create the need for constant monitoring and manipulation of foreign policy discourse in the governments of the region. These threats have always existed and are not likely to disappear in the near future.

My research question therefore is: *how the biopolitical concepts of security and survival shape the foreign policy discourses of the ruling elites of the South Caucasus states?*

Methodology

I have chosen Georgia, Armenia and Azerbaijan as examples to show that all three countries face similar external and internal problems. In Georgia, the competition between the West and Russia is more obvious, and the country's choices are clear. In general, Georgia needs to protect itself from Russian threats and occupation. Thus, for a country seeking peace and development, the West is an option.

In the case of Armenia, democratization and institution-building initiatives are helping the country move closer to the West. Noteworthy is the recent visit of U.S. House of Representatives speaker Nancy Pelosi to Yerevan. However, the Russian military presence in Armenia (Gyumri) and the ongoing Nagorno-Karabakh crisis limit the room for manoeuvre for the government of Nikol Pashinyan. Also, a strengthened Azerbaijan is the biggest threat to Armenia's national security.

Azerbaijan, rich in oil, is seeking to set up a steady export system to the EU and other Western markets. In addition, despite its victory in the Karabakh conflict, Baku is still not allowed to control parts of the territory. This has prompted the Aliyev administration to remain cautious of the Russian element inside the Nagorno-Karabakh conflict in order to preserve the neutrality of Russia which has increasingly distanced itself from Armenia since the Velvet Revolution of 2018.

The study uses the method of discourse analysis. Importantly, the paper explores the discourses of the Georgian ruling elite concerning relations with the EU and Russia. The time frame is substantial here: discourses are studied in the context of the Russian invasion of Georgia in 2008 and the Russian invasion of Ukraine in 2022. The political discourses of ruling elites in Azerbaijan and Armenia are explored in the setting of two escalations of the Nagorno-Karabakh conflict (2018 and 2020). For the analysis, the narratives of the ruling elites of these states on the existing threats and their foreign policy challenges are employed.

In every case, data is collected from interviews and other sources from local or global media, speeches, official statements and comments by senior government officials (Bidzina Ivanishvili and Irakli Gharibashvili from Georgia, Ilham Aliyev from Azerbaijan and Nikol Pashinyan from Armenia).

Conceptual Framework

Europeanization and Security: Perspectives of Elites

Europeanization is the process of bringing a country closer to the EU or its market. To some extent, Europeanization may take place within the framework of regional cooperation, such as the EaP. If a country wishes to become a member, the scope for Europeanization is even greater. Europeanization can also be understood as a desire to move closer to NATO. Georgia's desire to join the EU and/or NATO, Azerbaijan's special relationship with NATO's military power Türkiye and Armenia's reform plans create an essential environment for the Europeanization process. It should be noted that a constant sense of danger hinders the liberalization and democratization of existing forms of government in the countries of the region. Therefore, for the ruling elites, there are "temptations" to move towards authoritarianism.

Over the past three decades, theorists of Europeanization have studied the dynamics of the EU's eastward expansion. They have described this process as the simultaneous spread of Western institutions, values, markets, and prosperity in former socialist Europe. The conceptualization of Europeanization itself has in many cases been reduced to the participation of the target countries in the political dynamics of the EU (Ladrech 1994).

Featherstone and Kazamias (2001) point out that Europeanization is an iterative and dynamic process that manifests itself in the accession of various neighboring states to the EU. Here we must mention the several waves of EU enlargement that have been pursued since the collapse of the Warsaw Pact. However, prior to the infamous Russian invasion of Ukraine in 2022, there was considerable scepticism among Western scholars about the Europeanization process. Some scholars claimed that the EU was a gated community (Zaiotti 2007). However, with the granting of candidate country status to Ukraine and Moldova and the granting of the European perspective to Georgia, doubts about further eastern enlargement the EU has weakened.

According to Frank Schimmelfennig, the EU has the capacity for "external governance" which means that the EU imposes governance models and rules on external actors (Schimmelfennig 2010). Naturally, any country seeking to join the EU has an incentive to take advantage of the benefits offered by the EU for the improvement of the well-being of citizens. However, the process of association and accession also implies that the target country must follow the EU's recommendations and comply with its rules before it can benefit from them.

Europeanization implies a commitment to democracy, inter-party dialogue and institutional development. But the region is plagued by biopolitical discourses manipulated to consolidate power. The opportunity to consolidate power is exploited by governments. In other words, they manipulate the maintenance of their power in various ways, including:

1. Strong internal political polarization in Georgia and Armenia, between the current elite and the formers, where the formers (the UNM in Georgia or the Karabakh clan in Armenia) are accused by the current ones of being too radical in foreign policy and unable to avoid wars.
2. Authoritarianism in Azerbaijan, where the victorious President Aliyev avenged Azerbaijan's losses of the first Nagorno-Karabakh conflict after the escalation of 2020.

Biopolitics, History and Great Powers

The process of Europeanization in the South Caucasus is confronted with other major concerns that worry both the local governments and the population. These are ethnic conflicts and aggressive Russian interests which are often synthesized. Therefore, Europeanization, which is deeply linked to the concept of well-being, is confronted with the more urgent task of "survival". Europeanization is a long-term and planning-based process, and the task of survival requires less institutionalization and the production of quick decisions by elites. I argue that the conflict between these two concepts (Europeanization and survival) largely determines the formation of the existing political systems in the region.

For Foucault, the concept of biopolitics is directly related to the notion of survival of life (Foucault 1978). In a crisis situation when the ruling elite, the state, and the population are in imminent danger of losing their lives, it is logical for the ruling elite to base their power on the idea of survival. The concept of survival in the South Caucasus is still topical in the postmodern era. However, Soviet modernism in all three countries, most notably in Georgia and Armenia, strongly accentuates the ancientness of these nations and their survival after two millennia of the struggle between the mighty empires.

The historiography of Georgia and Armenia in the Soviet period stressed that both countries had survived several genocides and many wars of conquest. The Soviet period has been described as the age of prosperity and a post-historic phase for these countries. For instance, the popular four-volume scholarly work "Bare Swords" (Sanikidze 1989)on the history of Georgia states that during the two thousand-year history, Georgians did not even have the chance to rest and keep their swords in their sheaths.

The concept of survival for Armenians was linked to the damage caused by the Muslim invaders. The trauma was particularly acute and painful in the context of the Armenian genocide in the Ottoman Empire in 1915. In Georgia, the perception of the enemy after the tragedy of 9 April 1989 (Chikovani, et al. 2022) or perhaps decades earlier (Blauvelt 2018) has been that Russia is the major enemy of Georgians, rather than the Ottoman Empire and Iran. Remarkably, since the 1990s this attitude has intensified. The Abkhazian war and the ethnic cleansing of Georgians, which left nearly 8,000 Georgian civilians dead, imposed the same traumatic experiences on Georgians as those experienced by Armenians during the 1915 events in northeastern Türkiye.

The post-historicism that had dominated Soviet historiography in the South Caucasus republics thus ended in 1991, and traditional fears of survival emerged. In short, these fears are archaic, as they stem from a centuries-old tradition of self-victimization and struggle for true survival. Andrey Makarychev describes this phenomenon as „biopolitical patriotism" which does not imply the commitment of society to its government, although it is a powerful phenomena in itself (Makarychev and Yatsuk 2020). In my view, biopolitical patriotism can be the tool of governments in their quest to legitimise power in a moment of crisis.

In the case of Azerbaijan, which emerged victorious from the Nagorno-Karabakh conflict in 2020 and took revenge on Armenia, an enemy it accuses of ethnic cleansing, the notion of survival mingles with that of biopolitical patriotism and largely leads to the strengthening of Ilham Aliyev's power.

Russia's interests have a colossal influence on the dynamics of conflicts in the South Caucasus. The years between the collapse of the

Soviet Union and 2022, when Russia launched a full-scale war with Ukraine, have shown that Russia's foreign strategy does not shy away from directly or indirectly initiating bloody conflicts.

In the case of Georgia, Russia is a direct threat. In the case of Armenia and Azerbaijan, Russia is the central factor that has an interest in freezing the Nagorno-Karabakh conflict permanently and reactivating it at the appropriate time. Therefore, Russia's aggressive ambitions and associated risks influence the foreign policy priorities of the countries in the region.

In this study, the concept of survival is seen as an effort to preserve the lives of the people of Azerbaijan, Georgia and Armenia, for which the governments of these nations are responsible. The management of life-saving measures is referred to in biopolitical studies as "zoepolitics". Schinkel defines zoepolitics as a political structure that takes over the fight to save people's lives (Schinkel 2010).

Zoepolitics is the field of reflection in which the ruling elites of the three nations think and make decisions. The three states have varying degrees of aspiration towards the Western world. However, Russian efforts and threats (evident in the case of Georgia, but indirectly also in the case of Armenia-Azerbaijan) are forcing the elites to be more accommodating between their own foreign policy objectives and their actual capabilities. The probability of synthesizing zoepolitics with biopolitical patriotism is high in all three countries of the region. This, in turn, creates a path of consensus between the ruling elites and the population. This synthesis in itself implies an increase in the sovereignty and flexibility of the ruling elites in foreign policy matters, in a context of increased competition between the West and Russia. Also, zoepolitics can be read as the opportunity for local governments to manipulate with biopolitical patriotism and consolidate their power by marginalizing opposition and promoting illiberal rule through refusing liberal institutions.

Georgia: Comfortably Numb?

The debate on the Europeanization of the South Caucasus is reinforced by the recognition of Georgia's European perspective in 2022. Georgia has come a long way towards the EU and Western structures in general. It should be noted that this direction was clearly defined in

2003, after the Rose Revolution. The pursuit of EU and NATO membership has been central to the country's foreign policy agenda under both the previous government (UNM: 2003-2012) and the current government (GD: 2012-present). However, NATO's rejection of Georgia and Ukraine's accession at the Bucharest summit had far-reaching consequences, leading to the indefinite postponement of NATO membership. The most notable of these was the war that broke out in August 2008, which ended with Russia annexing large parts of Georgia and recognizing the power of the *de facto* separatist governments there.

The bombs dropped on Georgian cities greatly increased the feeling of insecurity. The prevailing public opinion was that this was Russian retaliation for Georgia's decision to integrate with the West. It is worth noting that on 12 August 2008, when the Russian invasion of Georgia was still in its hot phase and the threat of a military attack on Tbilisi was real, the leaders of five Eastern European countries (including Poland, Ukraine, Lithuania, Latvia and Estonia) arrived in Tbilisi on Rustaveli Avenue and joined a large peaceful demonstration. This was a symbolic gesture. If Tbilisi was in mortal danger, then the leaders of Eastern Europe could stand with the people against the Russian tanks and bombs. It should be noted that the tragic death of Polish President Lech Kaczynski in 2010 in a plane crash on Russian territory increased the sense of insecurity, on the one hand, and the perception of Russia as an aggressive and terrorist force, on the other, in Georgian society.

The intensification of energy projects and trade between the West and Russia, as well as Russia's accession to various international organizations, such as the World Trade Organization (in which Georgia also had to vote), reinforced the feeling that Russia was not required to pay a response for the 2008 war. As a result, space for the search for pragmatism emerged in Georgian society, followed by the emergence of GD as a large opposition coalition.

Bidzina Ivanishvili, the billionaire leader of GD, became the country's prime minister after winning the 2012 elections. It is worth noting that in 2013, in Riga, he publicly stated that he did not see Russia as a mortal threat: "I do not believe that Russia's strategy is to annex its neighbours" (Ivanishvili 2013).

This particular formulation of Russian-Georgian relations constituted the major part of the GD discourse in which the confrontation between Georgia and Russia was problematic. At the same time, Ivanishvili noted that Georgia did not have the resources for a full-scale "reconciliation" with Russia. However, the refusal to use harsh language would greatly help the country's security (Tabula 2013).

In 2014, following the events of Euromaidan, the Russian annexation of Crimea and the separatist war in eastern Ukraine, Ivanishvili assessed Russia's actions as a threat and a source of unrest in the region and the world. He noted, however, that Georgia must necessarily find a way to live with Russia and that this should not offend Russia as a state, despite the government's actions (Ivanishvili 2014).

Remarkably, Georgian leaders (Ivanishvili and Gharibashvili) often focus on the dangerous nature of Russia and perceive/present it as the deadly danger which can cause deadly results to Georgia. Thus, avoiding the danger is the central theme which GD uses in its "peace" discourse. This discourse has remained surprisingly consistent which can be further explained through the statements of Irakli Gharibashvili regarding the 2022 Russian annexation of Ukraine.

Russia continues to install barbed wire around "South Ossetia" by clandestinely moving the border further and further into Georgian territory which the Russian-led puppet regime calls "borderization" (Kakachia, et al. 2017). This issue still remains relevant in Georgia today. Although the period of open confrontation with Russia has passed, the occupation continues.

The consolidation and legitimacy of the power of GD depends to a large extent on its leaders' success in integrating biopolitics into the public discourse. The constant emphasis on peace by GD should be understood as an indication that the protection of Georgia from bombing, military annexation by Russia and the whole seriousness of the war situation is considered by the government as its own merit. On the other hand, the association with the EU is a big step towards integration with the EU, which to some extent falls within the realm of biopolitics. In particular, prosperity and wealth in the form of the EU is a safe space in biopolitical understanding and a direction for foreign engagement for Georgia.

The above statement by Bidzina Ivanishvili about Russia has been the epitome of the GD discourse for years. But the invasion of Ukraine in 2022 demands a clearer explanation of GD and its relationship with Russia.

The West's clear support for Ukraine is eroding the biopolitical formula that GD has been exploiting for years. This formula is designed to provide security from Russia, which GD sees as its main success, and thus reinforces the social contract[iii] with the Georgian people. Although the West did not impose the toughest sanctions on Russia until 2022, it consciously cut and isolated economic ties with Russia starting in February 2022. As a result, Western recognition of Georgia's economic ties with Russia changed from approval[iv] to suspicion.[v] Meanwhile, Georgia, previously lauded for its efforts to improve relations with Russia, became embroiled in diplomatic strife with the Ukrainian authorities after Prime Minister Gharibashvili refused to join the West's sanctions against Russia.

It should be noted that Irakli Gharibashvili responded to the issue of possible sanctions on the second day of the start of the Russian annexation of Ukraine and said the following:

> "I will not do anything, I will not take a single decision that will in any way damage the national interests of our country and the national interests of our people." (Gharibashvili 2022)."

It should be noted that in his statement of 25 February, Gharibashvili made a major point, noting that the sanctions were against Georgia's national interests. As time went on, the Prime Minister's statements became more and more clear. For example, on 3 April 2022, when tens of thousands of people gathered on Rustaveli Avenue in Tbilisi in support of Ukraine, the Prime Minister responded to this demonstration. First, he defended his decision and stressed that he was acting in the national interest. He then began to clarify what had been said.

> "Let's not forget, today our country is already invaded. We should behave more responsibly towards our people. We have lived through 3 wars in 30 years, in these wars, unfortunately, hundreds of people have suffered, tens of thousands of displaced people are in our country. This must stop, we must not repeat the mistakes, we must not be imprudent." (Gharibashvili 2022)

References to war, to past traumas and wounds, which could unfold at any moment are already built into these sentences. It should be noted that here the loyalty to the biopolitical language that has characterized GD from the first days of the rise to power has appeared. Gharibashvili, in particular, clearly emphasizes peace and says the following:

> "Our politics is peace-oriented and peace-based. We want peace, stability and development. This is what our country needs today. No one needs war, every patriotic government must do everything to avoid war, to avoid the greatest harm, which is war, from its own country and its own people. I will act in that spirit and with that responsibility (Gharibashvili 2022)."

Georgia has partially joined the financial sanctions against Russia (TASS Russian News Agency 2022). It has also voted for and sponsored the tough anti-Russian resolutions adopted by the United Nations (Georgia Today 2022). It also offers free asylum to refugees from Ukraine (Lomsadze 2022). However, the partial nature of sanctions, the non-closure of the border to Russian citizens (tens of thousands of Russian citizens have been living in Tbilisi since February) and the refusal to transfer military weapons to Ukraine (Agenda.ge 2022) have set a foreign policy agenda for Georgia that is partially divorced from the Western agenda.

In my opinion, this policy of the Georgian ruling elite is a typical example of what Schenkel calls zoepolitics. The emphasis on saving the lives of the Georgian population gave the Georgian authorities the opportunity to use the concept of biopolitical patriotism to their advantage.

This gave the Georgian government a certain sovereignty in the midst of a major international crisis. On the other hand, new obstacles have emerged. In particular, EU membership, which Georgia, Ukraine and Moldova had been waiting for since April, was granted to Ukraine and Moldova in June. Georgia was only granted a European perspective and had to implement reforms in order to obtain candidate status.

These obligations include reforms that risk deconstructing the existing power status quo in Georgia. In particular, reform of the judiciary system, depolarization and limiting the influence of Bidzina Ivanishvili in political decision-making are the key demands of the European Union (Jam-News 2022).

In a public speech announcing Georgia's application for EU membership in April, Gharibashvili referred to Europe as "Georgia's historical family" and noted that EU membership is a long-standing Georgian dream. However, after the European Commission suspended the candidate status, Gharibashvili said that Georgia was not granted this status only because there is no war between Russia and Georgia today. Gharibashvili said that candidate status was an encouragement to Ukraine, which is in the middle of a devastating war with Russia. It should be noted that the Georgian authorities announced soon that they planned to implement the EU recommendations as they aim to obtain the suspended status by the end of 2022.

The debate between Georgia and the EU is still in full effect. There are only a few months left to decide if Georgia will join Ukraine and Moldova as EU candidates.

On the other hand, the war, with all of its biopolitical dimensions, has made it easier for Georgia's ruling elite to surmount the hurdle of a partial EU rejection (which would have been impossible in another context, since for the Georgian society European prosperity and peace are in the same biopolitical categories).

The emphasis on peace and the amount of damage in Ukraine, on the other hand, have fueled Georgian biopolitical patriotism. GD sees the temporary denial of EU candidate status as a punishment for pursuing a moderate policy towards Russia.[vi] Despite this, the party is promoting reforms and says it will do its utmost to obtain candidate status. Biopolitical concepts such as saving life are the language through which GD speaks to the Georgian public. Media footage of the devastation and information about the loss of life coming from Ukraine confirms long-standing fears in Georgia. Accordingly, Georgia's foreign policy discourse has become more autonomous vis-à-vis the EU, influenced by biopolitical notions of security and survival.

Armenia: Capacities versus Limits

In the case of Armenia, the debate on the proximity of the EU and Armenia is obscured by the presence of Russia as the pillar of Armenia's security. However, the debate is still topical in the light of the Velvet Revolution and the 2018 reforms. Especially if we start from adequate hypotheses that Europeanization and democratization are parallel processes, combined by the transformative power of the EU (Grabbe 2006).

Georgia is the most advanced country in the South Caucasus region in terms of integration with the EU. However, it should be noted that Armenia is making important steps in this direction. Above all, the 2017 Comprehensive and Enhanced Partnership Agreement (CEPA) should be mentioned. In recent years, Armenia has also seen an increase in the number of people wishing to join the EU; this share now stands at 40% of the population.

On the other hand, Armenia is a member of the EAEU and is highly dependent on Russia for both trade and security.

Security issues in Armenia have a major impact on the political life of the country. In particular, the issue of national security is closely linked to the 30-year Nagorno-Karabakh conflict. The Nagorno-Karabakh conflict has been an obstacle to Armenia's development for many years and has made the country completely dependent on the Russian Federation and its arms supplies. Between 1999 and 2018, Armenia was ruled by the so-called "Karabakh Clan" whose central representatives were former leaders of state Robert Kocharian and Serzh Sargsyan.

The Karabakh Clan is now associated with stagnation, oligarchic rule and corruption in Armenia. However, before the Velvet Revolution of 2018, the clan was in a strong position and had full control of the state. The main reason for this is the discourse of security and survival, which the clan used effectively in the Nagorno-Karabakh issue. In particular, the Clan stressed that its relations and actions with Russia were aimed at securing Nagorno-Karabakh's freedom from Azerbaijan.

To this day, Armenian society still largely believes that the world has turned a blind eye to the injustices committed against the country (Redstate 2022) and that Armenians are struggling to survive. In this context, the experience of the 1915 genocide is particularly noteworthy because of its profound impact on the Armenian nation's external relations in the world of the present time (Policy Perspectives 2016).

It is worth noting that the new government formed in Armenia in 2018 is in line with the broad opinion of Armenian society on the Nagorno-Karabakh issue (Zartonk News Agency 2020). The

Pashinyan regime has revolutionary plans in the areas of governance, democracy and anti-corruption. However, on the issue of Nagorno-Karabakh, it is no different from the previous regime. The apocalyptic rhetoric about saving Armenians, which mainly refers to maintaining Armenian military control over Nagorno-Karabakh, has not changed during the first two years of the Pashinyan's government.

In 2019, during a visit to the capital of Nagorno-Karabakh, Nikol Pashinyan said: "Artsakh (the Armenian name for Nagorno-Karabakh) and Armenia should unite" (Kucera 2019). During the same address to the population of Stepankert, Pashinyan underlined that "Artsakh is Armenia, and period" (OC Media 2019).

Many experts believe that he did so in order to win a domestic political battle. In particular, the Karabakh Clan and the previous Armenian government have alluded to his soft stance on Nagorno-Karabakh. This is why Pashinyan had to comply with the prevailing ideas of security and survival and offer this proposal to the Karabakh Armenians.

The formal reunification of Armenia and separatist Nagorno-Karabakh would be an event of global significance. It should be noted that there are no supporters of this idea in the West or in Russia. The idea of liberating Karabakh's Armenians from Azerbaijan is entirely biopolitical, and liberating them literally means bodily survival. Thus, in the context of Armenian mobilization, Pashinyan's statement carries a lot of weight. It is noteworthy that the Georgian government is using biopolitical language to avoid being drawn into the huge regional crisis between Russia and Ukraine. On the other hand, Pashinyan's biopolitical discourse became one of the reasons for the escalation of the conflict in 2020, before which the Azerbaijani state was alarmed by Pashinyan's statements.

The foreign policy agenda set by the Armenian state under the government of Nikol Pashinyan can be divided into two phases. The first runs from the 2018 revolution to the large-scale escalation of the war in 2020. The second phase runs from the 2020 war to the present.

The years 2018-2020 are the years of Armenia's Europeanization. During this period, Pashinyan has openly pointed out that "the task of the Armenian state is to move closer to the European Union" (ARKA News Agency 2018).[vii] He also opposed Armenia's membership of the EAEU before coming to power. During his visits to several EU countries and in various forums and public statements, the Armenian authorities emphasized civil society, the rule of law and other liberal concepts. Clearly, there was a double game—on the one hand, staying in the EAEU and on the other hand, the path of reforms typical of the classical velvet revolutions could not coexist.

Russia's indirect support (disguised as diplomatic neutrality) for Armenia in Nagorno-Karabakh degenerated into *de facto* neutrality since 2018. This was instrumental in making Armenia stand by itself against a strengthened Azerbaijani army in autumn 2020. I think this was Russia's punishment for the dual game initiated by Pashinyan.

Pashinyan managed to gain domestic legitimacy by manipulating biopolitical concepts before the escalation of the war. During the 2018-2020 period, the West's position was a peaceful resolution of the conflict, with Russia as a guarantor of genuine peace. After 2020, concepts of security and survival shifted from being manipulated by Armenia's ruling elite to being manipulative towards Armenia's ruling elite.

To put it more clearly, the Europeanization and reforms of the years 2018-2020 have been overshadowed by the new reality created by the war in Karabakh in 2020. The Armenian ruling elite could no longer play a double game and had to be guided by the needs of security and survival.

As the idea of rapprochement with the EU faded into the background, Armenia welcomed the idea of a 3+3 format.[viii] The 3+3 format is seen as a regional cooperation between the three big (Russia, Türkiye, Iran) and three small (Georgia, Armenia, Azerbaijan) countries of the Caucasus region which in practice creates geopolitical hegemony of the three big countries. Thereby, the EU conciliation discourse launched by Armenia was shelved for reasons of security and survival. Armenia's attempt to play the double game has ended in Russia's favor. In this context, it is worth noting that a ceasefire agreement was signed between Armenia and Azerbaijan on November 9, 2020 (Moscow time), brokered by President Putin.

After the 2020 war, Armenia actively sought military support from both Russia and the Russian-led Collective Security Treaty Organization (CSTO). For example, in May 2022, at the organization's summit, Pashinyan called for the deployment of troops to protect Armenians (Babayan 2022). Pashinyan was referring to the border conflict between Armenia and Azerbaijan (outside Nagorno-Karabakh).

Remarkably, Pashinyan has also underlined the "special role" (Asbarez 2022) of Russia in the 2020 ceasefire. In brief, the security and peace concerns that arose from the Nagorno-Karabakh war in 2020 led to a shift in Armenia's post-revolution foreign policy discourse from pro-Western to authentic and traditionally neutrality-oriented. The starting point for this is that the Russian-Armenian rapprochement did not become the basis of widespread protest. On the contrary, Pashinyan's zoepolitics significantly enhanced his domestic legitimacy which was confirmed by the victory of Pashinyan's party in the early elections of 2021.

Azerbaijan: Ways of Questioning Russian Domination

If we consider Azerbaijan as a cultural and identity enclave of Türkiye in the South Caucasus, then it is natural to associate Azerbaijan with the Europeanization process. First of all, former Azerbaijani President Elchibey's concept of "two states, one nation" remains valid and is reflected in the close cooperation between Ankara and Baku. Secondly, Türkiye continues to maintain its status as a candidate for EU membership and has not renounced it. In addition, Türkiye is integrated into the West as a member of NATO and shares borders with the EU.

Azerbaijan has advantages that make it the most attractive country in the South Caucasus region. These are, first and foremost, its energy reserves and economic resilience. On the other hand, Azerbaijan, like the other two countries in the region, is entangled in Russia's power games and tragic regional conflicts. Therefore, the biopolitical discourse is strong here as well.

Azerbaijan's victory in Nagorno-Karabakh in 2020 is a story of "revenge": in the 1990s, the Armenians organized ethnic cleansing against the Azerbaijanis and even occupied areas bordering Karabakh to create a buffer zone. The resulting trauma of defeat and appeal to genocide by the Armenians united Azerbaijani society for years.

On the other hand, Armenians often refer to Azerbaijanis as Turks. This is to emphasize the kinship and common origin of these two nations. The nature of this emphasis is biopolitical: the Ottoman

Turks killed up to one million Armenians in the 1915 genocide, and the Armenians point to the same threat from Azerbaijan in the Karabakh War.

The Black Sea links Georgia to the EU countries Bulgaria and Romania, but also to candidate Ukraine which is specifically important for Georgia's accession to the EU. In the case of Azerbaijan, geography is an obstacle. In particular, Azerbaijan belongs to the Caspian Sea basin and has not yet fully defined its rights in this oil-rich sea.

On the other hand, Azerbaijan, like Georgia, sees Russia as a threat rather than a partner. Here, first of all, we should refer to the role that Russia played in the first Nagorno-Karabakh war in supplying Armenia with weapons. Armenia has been perceived as a death threat for Azerbaijan since 1991. The anti-Armenian discourse and the defeat in the first Karabakh conflict led Azerbaijan to seek a reliable foreign partner. That partner is Türkiye.

First, Azerbaijanis and Turks (i.e. the majority of the population of these countries) are ethnically related. Secondly, Azerbaijanis and Turks speak largely the same language; the difference is in the dialect.

Thirdly, after the collapse of the Soviet Union, Türkiye started looking for partners in the region. Despite difficult past experiences with Armenia and Georgia, Türkiye has managed to develop peaceful neighborly relations with Georgia. However, the greatest success has been achieved with Azerbaijan.

Following the 2020 Karabakh War, Stepankert, the capital of the separatist republic, became an enclave with Russian troops controlling the narrow Lachin corridor that connects Armenia with The Nagono-Karabakh. Otherwise, the entire Armenian part of The Nagorno-Karabakh is surrounded by Azerbaijan.

The problem of enclaves is also present in Azerbaijan. This is the Autonomous Republic of Nakhchivan, which is part of Azerbaijan, although it does not have a direct border with the mainland. Armenia separates Nakhichevan from Azerbaijan from the east. However, to the west Nakhichevan borders Türkiye which enhances Turkish influence over Nakhichevan and Azerbaijan as a whole.

For decades, the Nagorno-Karabakh problem has been a constant threat to Azerbaijan. Survival and security concepts played a central role and ensured the strengthening of Azerbaijan's military power, which could deal with security issues. Azerbaijan, on the other hand, has an important ally in this biopolitical struggle in the form of Türkiye, a major NATO military power. However, Türkiye is only partially integrated with the West, as the country has been denied membership in the EU for decades.

As a result, Türkiye is more of a gateway to the EU market for Azerbaijan than a factor bringing Azerbaijan closer to the West. Moreover, unlike Armenia and Georgia, Azerbaijan is not interested in becoming a liberal democracy, and the EU serves the country more as a market than as an ultimate goal.

As long as the Nagorno-Karabakh conflict remains unresolved (parts of the region, including the capital, are still under Armenian control), Azerbaijan will remain under constant threat. Moreover, Russia is rightly seen as Armenia's ally in this conflict.

Azerbaijan, therefore, needs continued reinforcement and economic growth. Only then will the country be able to deal with security issues properly. Victory in the 2020 war has partially eliminated Azerbaijan's self-image as a victim. But security problems remain. Thus, the EU should be seen both as a balancing factor to help Azerbaijan deal with Russian interests and manipulation in the region, and as a market where Azerbaijan's oil is sold and from where Azerbaijan can continue its economic growth.

Today, most of the exports from Azerbaijan go to the EU. Here, first of all, energy resources are meant, which in the background of the current war between Russia and Ukraine, has acquired even more importance. Azerbaijan is a member state of the EaP since 2009. However, EU-Azerbaijan relations were more problematic in the previous decade than they are now.

It should be noted that in 2019, Ilham Aliyev said that "Türkiye is not accepted in the EU only because it is a Muslim state" (Rehimov 2019).

On the other hand, the relationship between the EU and Azerbaijan is developing in parallel with growing trade. The EU's foreign direct investment in Azerbaijan has now reached $8 billion. It should be noted that the EU is financing Azerbaijan's institutional development and the career development of civil servants. Aliyev said in 2019 that Azerbaijan would not campaign for EU membership (2019). But the dynamics of relations show that the states are becoming close partners.

Trade with the EU as the largest oil market has had a positive impact on Azerbaijan's economic growth and security. If we say that the successes in Nagorno-Karabakh are due to Azerbaijan's financial strength, it is clear that the EU has a big role to play here too. Without trade with the EU, Azerbaijan would find it difficult to achieve such economic success.

The concluding perspective of the analysis of Azerbaijan-EU relations is the regional competition between the West and Russia. In particular, Russia's invasion of Ukraine in 2022 has seriously harmed Russia's role as a mediator in the Nagorno-Karabakh conflict. Russia's international isolation is a serious blow to Moscow's prestige.

Interestingly, Pashinyan and Aliyev met in Brussels in 2022. The mediator was the President of the European Council, Charles Michel. Charles Michel stressed that it is necessary to find ways and means for peaceful coexistence between Armenia and Azerbaijan (Press Release 2022). For this purpose, he noted, it is necessary to build trust between these two states. Michel also mentioned joint projects that can bring the two states closer. In light of Russia's unjustified attack on Ukraine and the massacre of civilians, Michel's peace message promotes EU support in the strained relations between Armenia and Azerbaijan.

Moreover, Russia's power and influence today are based solely on its military strength, the possible peace deal between Armenia and Azerbaijan threatens the prevailing discourses on security and survival, over which Russia has great influence. Even more, against the backdrop of the war in Ukraine, Armenia's "return" to the Russian orbit is still fragile, and the Pashinyan government, which enjoys new legitimacy, has the option of seeking other foreign platforms to obtain security guarantees. Given Azerbaijan's close relations with the EU, these guarantees and the likelihood of finding the necessary platform are realistic.

In May 2022, following a meeting with European MPs in Brussels, Ilham Aliyev stated that he was grateful to the EU for mediating Armenian-Azerbaijani problems. Aliyev said:

"The European Union has played an important role in normalizing relations between Armenia and Azerbaijan." (Interfax 2022)[ix]

This leaves room for changing the function of the Nagorno-Karabakh arbitrator and "appointing" the EU instead of Russia. The introduction of the EU into the Nagorno-Karabakh conflict has shown that foreign policy discourses in the region are fragile and Russia's positions are largely based on military power and the threats it makes. On the other hand, the possible weakening of Russia against the backdrop of the war in Ukraine means the strengthening of other major players in the region. This could easily be the EU.

Interestingly, in the case of Georgia and Armenia, the conflicts and threats come from "stronger" opponents. In the case of Georgia, this is a disproportionately strong Russia; in the case of Armenia, it is the Ankara-Baku tandem that defeated Armenia in Nagorno-Karabakh in 2020. So, in the case of Georgia and Armenia, the survival and security discourses are continuous and do not reach the "end" or triumph, at which point the sense of danger either disappears or diminishes significantly. Azerbaijan's victory in the 2020 war, as well as in subsequent smaller escalations in 2021 and 2022, was attributed exclusively to Ilham Aliyev, who is far more influential in Azerbaijan than Pashinyan in Armenia or Gharibashvili in Georgia. Moreover, there is hardly any opposition camp and no political polarization or plurality in Azerbaijan. Consequently, survival and security concepts could only interact with the concept of triumph in Azerbaijan, where Aliyev's authority and power are even stronger than before. In 2022, for example, Aliyev addressed the population with the following words:

> "From now on, the people of Azerbaijan will live as a victorious people, live forever, and our state will live as a victorious state from now on. This is a great happiness for all of us, for those living in Azerbaijan, for Azerbaijani citizens, for Azerbaijanis living abroad." (Aliyev 2022)

Conclusion

The need for security and survival within a belligerent West-Russia context is of particular relevance to Georgia, where GD as the ruling party needs to demonstrate a commitment to reform in the light of the European perspective adopted in June 2022. However, the Georgian government is also committed to pursue a parallel policy of peace and trade with Russia.

For the longest time, GD had thus been seeking to balance the proclaimed long-term Europeanization agenda with the immediate Russian threat in order to keep the country from being drawn into a conflict between the West and Russia. The search for this balance reinforces the role of biopolitical discourse, which the ruling party uses to seek public legitimacy and to consolidate its power through elections. Georgia has been exploiting this equilibrium for a decade. However, after the annexation of Ukraine (2014 and 2022), biopolitical concepts such as survival and security have taken on greater importance.

In Armenia, the intertwining of the reform agenda with the Turkish-Azerbaijani threat has forced the Armenian government to recognize and accept the constraints imposed on the country by the geopolitical environment. As a result, Westernization and Europeanization of Armenia are growing. It should also be noted that Russia has less time for the South Caucasus due to the ongoing war in Ukraine. However, it is still present with military bases in Georgia (Abkhazia and South Ossetia) and Armenia (Gyumri) and remains an important player. Pashinyan's "equilibrium", strengthened by early parliamentary elections in 2021, assumes reform of the country and a rapprochement with the EU and the United States in the future, although this is limited by the future threat from Azerbaijan, which is forcing the country to maintain engagement with Russia.

The task of saving Karabakh Armenians from ethnic cleansing (the separatist capital of Stepankert is surrounded by Azerbaijan) and protecting the Armenian-Azerbaijani border contributes to the relevance of the concepts of security and survival. Thus, the Pashinyan regime can play a double game of friendship with an increasingly unnecessary Russia and the regionally emerging West that was a central supporter of the 2018 Velvet Revolution.

After the war in 2020, the "Armenian threat" in Azerbaijan was largely subdued. Ilham Aliyev, the least democratic but most consolidated leader in the region, is the main guarantor of Azerbaijan's security and survival after the victory of the war.

Aliyev has successfully reconciled Azerbaijan's security and survival challenges by keeping Russia's active intervention in the 2020 Armenia-Azerbaijan conflict at bay and maintaining dialogue with Russia, while making it possible for Azerbaijan to build a regional oil pipeline to Europe (despite Russian unsatisfaction) and getting closer to Türkiye, striking an equalibrium that successfully balances Azerbaijan's security and survival challenges. This balance is a biopolitical mechanism that presupposes the maintenance and growth of the legitimacy of Aliyev's government.

Bibliography

Agenda.ge. 2022. *Parliament Speaker: Military Aid to Ukraine, Opening Second Front are Questions Georgia Cannot Take Part In*. Tbilisi, April 29. https://agenda.ge/en/news/2022/1500.

Aliyev, Ilham. 2022. *President Ilham Aliyev: From Now On, The People of Azerbaijan Will Live as a Victorious People*. April 22. https://azerbaijan.az/en/news/9290.

ARKA News Agency. 2018. *Armenia to Deepen Relations with European Union, Pashinyan Says*. Yerevan, May 9. https://arka.am/en/news/politics/armenia_to_deepen_relations_with_european_union_pashinyan_says_/.

Asbarez. 2022. "Putin, Pashinyan Cement Russia's 'Key' Role in Karabakh Settlement." *Asbarez*. April 19. https://asbarez.com/putin-pashinyan-cement-russias-key-role-in-karabakh-settlement/.

Babayan, Aza. 2022. "The Armenian Mirror Spectator." *Pashinyan Again Criticizes Russian-Led Military Bloc*. May 17. https://mirrorspectator.com/2022/05/17/pashinyan-again-criticizes-russian-led-military-bloc/.

Blauvelt, Timothy. 2018. *Georgia after Stalin: Nationalism and Soviet Power*. New York: Routledge.

Chikovani, Nino, Ketevan Kakitelashvili, Ivane Tsereteli, Irakli Chkhaidze, Maia Kvrivishvili, and Ketevan Epadze. 2022. *Georgia: Trauma and Triumph on the Way to Independence*. Tbilisi.

Foucault, Michel. 1978. *The History of Sexuality*. New York: Random House. Inc.

Georgia Today. 2022. *Georgia Co-sponsors UN Security Council Vetoed By Russia*. Tbilisi, February 26. https://georgiatoday.ge/georgia-co-sponsors-un-security-council-resolution-vetoed-by-russia/.

Gharibashvili, Irakli. 2022. *Sanctions Will Not be Imposed, Don't Forget, Today our Country is Occupied.* Tbilisi, April 3.

Gharibashvili, Irakli. 2022. *We Will Not Join the Sanctions Imposed on Russia.* Tbilisi, February 25.

Grabbe, Heather. 2006. *The EU's Transformative Power: Europeanization Through Conditionality in Central and Eastern Europe.* New York: Palgrave Macmillan.

2019. "Ilham Aliyev—Azerbaijan is Not Going to Join The EU." *1tv.ge.* December 31. https://1tv.ge/lang/en/news/ilham-aliyev-azerbaijan-is-not-going-to-join-the-eu/.

Interfax. 2022. "Interfax: International Information Group." *Aliyev Praises EU's Role in Normalizing Azerbaijan's Relations with Armenia.* May 25. https://interfax.com/newsroom/top-stories/79548/.

Ivanishvili, Bidzina, interview by Olga Babluani. 2014. *A Farewell To Arms: Interview with Bidzina Ivanishvili* Georgian Public Broadcaster. December 22. Accessed November 1, 2022. https://www.youtube.com/watch?v=RPRRqGHUcek.

Ivanishvili, Bidzina, interview by Radio Palitra. 2013. *I Do Not Believe that Russia's Strategy is to Annex it's Neighbours* Tabula, (June 4). http://tbl.ge/4u34.

Jam-News. 2022. *Georgian NGOs Present a Plan for Obtaining EU Candidate Status.* Tbilisi, July 4. https://jam-news.net/georgian-ngos-present-a-plan-for-obtaining-eu-candidate-status/.

Kakachia, Kornely', Levan Kakhishvili, Joseph Larsen, and Mariam Grigalashvili. 2017. *Mitigating Russia's Borderization of Georgia: A Strategy to Contain and Engage.* Policy Paper, Tbilisi: Georgian Institute of Politics.

Kucera, Joshua. 2019. "Pashinyan Calls for Unification between Armenia and Karabakh." August 6. https://eurasianet.org/pashinyan-calls-for-unification-between-armenia-and-karabakh.

Ladrech, Robert. 1994. "Europeanization of Domestic Politics and Institutions: The Case of France." *Journal of Common Market Studies* 32 (1): 69-88.

Lomsadze, Giorgi. 2022. *Georgians Come to the Aid of Ukrainian Refugees.* Tbilisi, April 27. https://eurasianet.org/georgians-come-to-the-aid-of-ukrainian-refugees.

Makarychev, Andrey, and Alexandra Yatsuk. 2020. *Critical Biopolitics and Post-Soviet: From Populations to Nations.* Lanham, Maryland: Lexington Books.

Netgazeti. 2012. "What will be the Foreign-political Relations of The "Dream"." *Netgazeti*, August 31. https://netgazeti.ge/news/15616/.

OC Media. 2019. *https://oc-media.org/pashinyan-calls-for-unification-between-nagorno-karabakh-and-armenia/*. August 7. https://oc-media.org/pashinyan-calls-for-unification-between-nagorno-karabakh-and-armenia/.

Policy Perspectives. 2016. *Turning a Blind Eye: The US Failure to Recognize the Armenian Genocide After 101 Years.* Edited by Andre Avanessians. April 13. https://policy-perspectives.org/2016/04/13/turning-a-blind-eye-the-us-failure-to-recognize-the-armenian-genocide-after-101-years/.

Press Release. 2022. "Armenia-Azerbaijan: Leaders Meet President Michel and Agree to Work Towards Peace Treaty." *EU Neighbours East.* April 7. https://euneighbourseast.eu/news/latest-news/armenia-azerbaijan-leaders-meet-president-michel-and-agree-to-work-towards-peace-treaty/.

Redstate. 2022. *Will the World Turn a Blind Eye Again? Armenia Says At Least 49 Soldiers Were Killed in Attacks by Azerbaijan.* Edited by Levon Satamian. September 13. https://redstate.com/levon/2022/09/13/will-the-world-turn-a-blind-eye-again-armenia-says-at-least-49-soldiers-were-killed-in-attacks-by-azerbaijan-n606413.

Rehimov, Ruslan. 2019. "Azerbaijan Slams Delay in Turkey's EU Membership." *Anadolu Agency.* December 24. https://www.aa.com.tr/en/europe/azerbaijan-slams-delay-in-turkey-s-eu-membership/1682252.

Sammut, D. 2008. *A future Vision for the Caucasus-Caspian Region and its European Dimension.* European Policy Center Report.

Sanikidze, Levan. 1989. *Bare Swords.* Tbilisi: Merani.

Schimmelfennig, Frank. 2010. "Europeanisation Beyond the Member States." *Zeitschrift für Staats- und Europawissenschaften (ZSE) / Journal for Comparative Government and European Policy* (Nomos Verlagsgesellschaft mbH) 8 (3): 319-339.

Schinkel, Willem. 2010. "From Zoepolitics to Biopolitics: Citizenship and Construction of Society." *European Journal of Social Theory* 13 (2): 155-172.

Tabula. 2013. *Ivanishvili: I Can't Believe that Russia's Strategy is to Conquer and Occupy the Territories of Neighboring Countries.* Tbilisi, June 4.

TASS Russian News Agency. 2022. *Georgia Joins Ukraine-related Financial Sanctions Against Russia.* Tbilisi, April 1. https://www.bing.com/search?q=Georgia+joins+Ukraine-related+financial+sanctions+against+Russia&cvid=940258ec53ce414496902fb6e28cbd94&aqs=edge..69i57j69i64.302j0j4&FORM=ANAB01&PC=U531.

Zaiotti, Ruben. 2007. "Of Friends and Fences: Europe's Neighbourhood Policy and the 'Gated Community Syndrome." *Journal of European Integration* 29 (2): 143-162.

Zartonk News Agency. 2020. *An Overwhelming Majority Of Armenians Want The Unification Of Artsakh With Armenia.* July. https://zartonkmedia.com/2020/07/02/an-overwhelming-majority-of-armenians-want-the-unification-of-artsakh-with-armenia/.

---

[i] It should be noted that the process of creeping occupation, which has barely stopped after 2008 and which Russia and the separatist regions call "border demarcation", is causing significant damage to the Georgian population in the conflict zones. In addition to the division of villages by barbed wire and the frequent occupation of graveyards and pastures in the occupied territories, numerous cases of killings have been recorded. For example, near the border of occupied Abkhazia, a 'border guard' of the Russian forces deliberately killed a Georgian citizen, Giga Otkhozoria. Archil Tatunashvili, detained by the Ossetians, was tortured to death in the detention camp in Tskhinvali. All of this shows that the conflict is in a 'passive' phase and therefore the 'success' of the settlement of relations with Russia has rather sharp limits.

[ii] Since the beginning of the 20th century, many Armenians and Azerbaijanis have often seen each other as fierce enemies, willing to resort to physical murder and ethnic annihilation. Before the Soviet occupation of Armenia and Azerbaijan, there were several notorious pogroms in the South Caucasus in which Armenians and Azerbaijanis were engaged against each other. The rivalry is therefore deeply rooted in history.

[iii] It should be noted that since 2012, the Georgian Dream has repeatedly blamed the United National Movement for its passionate foreign policy that led to Russian aggression in 2008. On August 8, 2022, the fourteenth anniversary of the five-day August War, Prime Minister Gharibashvili openly accused former President Mikheil Saakashvili of "failing to prevent" the 2008 war and of "sacrificing the population and the military".

[iv] For instance, Geneva (Switzerland) has hosted up to 56 dialogue meetings between Georgia and Russia. In which, parallely with the problematic cases, the opportunities of economic cooperation were discussed.

[v] It should be noted that the emphasis on the concept of oligarchy in the resolution on Georgia presupposes the existence of a post-Soviet network of oligarchs. Therefore, in this resolution, Bidzina Ivanishvili is not considered a separate oligarch, but a member of this network, which is in open conflict with the West and supports Russia.
https://reginfo.ge/politics/item/26929-saakashvilis-provokaziulma-nabijebma-ganapiroba-is,-rom-omi-tavidan-ver-aiziles-%C3%A2%E2%82%AC%E2%80%9C-garibashvili

[vi] David Magradze is a famous Georgian poet and an author of Georgia's national anthem (since 2003) who is associated with 'The Georgian Dream''. During his interview at government supportive 'Imedi TV' he held that 'Georgia was punished with the denial of EU candidacy for not opening the second front against Russia' see:

[vii] http://primetime.ge/news/politika/dagvsajes-imitom-rom-meore-fronti-ar-gav khsenit-rats-chventvis-tvitganadgurebis-tolfasi-iqneboda-davit-maghradze
Remarkably, in May 2018, Pashinyan announced a rapprochement with the EU from Stephankert (the capital of Nagorno-Karabakh, still controlled by the Armenian side regardless of the 2020 military defeat). Armenia to deepen relations with European Union, Pashinyan says (arka.am).

[viii] *"Armenia will participate in "3+3 format"meeting on December 10"* Armenpress. 8 december 2021. https://armenpress.am/eng/news/1070268.html

[ix] https://interfax.com/newsroom/top-stories/79548/

EU-Armenia Relations as a Test Case for International Relations Theories

Diana R. Galoyan and Albert A. Hayrapetyan

Abstract

IR theories focus on states as key actors in the foreign policy arena. The EU, by comparison, emerged as a *sui generis* entity, making it necessary to develop new EU-intrinsic IR theories. In this chapter we will use the case of EU-Armenia relations to contribute to the scholarly discussions explaining EU external action policies through the prism of mixing and combining IR theories. The purpose of this chapter is threefold: to showcase the relevant theories and identify their inherent limitations, to develop an "interparadigm dialogue" by comparing and contrasting IR theories, and finally to reflect on EU external action policies through the application of the relevant IR theories by focusing on the example of EU-Armenia relations. We find that liberal intergovernmentalism in combination with the EU external governance theory may guide us to better understand the considerations of the politicians in charge of the EU external action policy.

Keywords: EU-Armenia relations; IR theories; Interparadigm dialogue; Realism; Liberalism; EU external governance theory; Social constructivism.

Introduction

Compared to states, the EU is a *sui generis* creation. In fact, never before did IR theories have to grapple with an entity woven around both intergovernmental and supranational institutions that emerged as a result of the free and voluntary relinquishment of sovereignty by states. By comparison, regional integration in other parts of the world is still in its embryonic stage. In other words, as the EU is the only regional cooperation format which is evolving from an intergovernmental to a supranational one, it poses new challenges to established theories on international relations.

This chapter will reflect on the EU external relations regarding Armenia from a theoretical point of view. It will showcase the relevant theories, identify their inherent shortcomings and develop an "interparadigm dialogue" by comparing and contrasting the relevant approaches. Armenia serves as a case in point because it is the only country that entered into economic (Eurasian Economic Union, EAEU) and military (Collective Security Treaty Organization, CSTO) integration formats with states without sharing a common border with any one of them. In fact, Armenia is the only Eastern Partnership (EaP) country that is a member of a Russia-led economic union and security architecture. The 2020 tragic war in Karabakh and its sizable human and military losses made the country even more vulnerable. Azerbaijan and Turkey closed the borders from east and west, and the skirmishes on the border with Azerbaijan became the "new normal" for the country. For that reason, in consideration of its security consideration, the country found itself at a watershed about 10 years ago—EU or Russia. Therefore, while the case is not generalizable, it may serve as a "laboratory" to test the relevant IR theories and their explanatory power.

In order to determine which particular mix of IR theories is best suited to explain the nature of EU-Armenia relations, the following theories will be examined: realism & neo-realism, federalism, neo-functionalism, liberal intergovernmentalism, European external governance theory and social constructivism. The rationale behind this choice is the following: realism (rarely discussed in the context of European integration), liberalism (and consequently liberal-intergovernmentalism, as it is just one branch of liberal IR theories) and constructivism are well established IR theories, also known as the "grand theories". They lay claim to explicate the considerations behind almost any interstate affair and they will remain pertinent to the field of European integration at least as long as the Treaties (for example the Lisbon Treaty) are signed by "High Contracting Parties". On the other hand, EU external governance theory lays claim to explicate the power projection of the EU beyond its borders.

Interparadigm Dialogue

Realism, as the oldest school of IR, significantly predates European integration. Therefore, in this context the first research question shall be amended slightly as follows: how could European integration possibly be interpreted though the lens of a realist scholar? The shortest answer would be—there is no and cannot be European integration! Let's see why.

Nicollò Machiavelli, in his celebrated seminal oeuvre "The Prince", gives a set of commandments on effective implementation of power-oriented politics (Machiavelli 1532). Having cherished the dream to unite the then-scattered Italian city states under the same polity and, most probably, bearing Lorenzo de Medici of Florence in mind for that historical mission, he would hardly imagine any prince to unite the bulk of Europe in a way other than by military conquest, let alone by voluntary relinquishment of a considerable part of sovereignty by 28 sovereigns to any kind of supranational formation. Almost a century later, British philosopher Hobbes, another prominent forerunner of the modern-day realists, considered war as a natural condition of human being (Hobbes 1651, 76-79). The two mentioned seminal works later became major philosophical inspiration for the modern-day realists among whom Hans J. Morgenthau defined the following six principles of realism:

1. The government of politics by rational laws rooted in the nature of human being.
2. Ensuring the national interests by means of accruing more power.
3. The variable nature of state interests.
4. Inapplicability of the universal moral principles to state foreign policy.
5. Disguising the actions of the nations under the universal moral principles.
6. The autonomy of IR, i.e. political realism, unlike other disciplines defines interest differently (Morgenthau 1948).

Among the modern-day realists, John Mearsheimer foreboded the collapse of European integration. In particular, he stated that the realm of peace on the old continent was a corollary of the following factors: a bipolar world, the presence of nuclear weapons and distribution of power among the poles with the latter being the most important factor (Mearsheimer 1990, 10-31). As for the polarity, he avers that the presence of multiple poles leaves a room for maneuvers that might entail a miscalculation, and war is inevitable for guaranteeing security. As for nuclear balance, his arguments, largely shared by another (defensive) neo-realist Kenneth Waltz (Waltz and Sagan 2013), are mostly about the deterring effect of nuclear weapons. In addition, he gives due credit to the role of nationalism as a source of mobilization for war (Mearsheimer 1990, 20).

Mearsheimer believed the Soviet's departure from the Old continent will pave the way for one the following four scenarios: 1. Europe without nuclear weapons, 2. Europe with no further proliferation, 3. well-managed nuclear proliferation and 4. not well-managed nuclear proliferation (Sagan and Waltz 2013, 33-40). All those scenarios would be fraught with dangers. For instance, in the case of "Europe without nuclear power", the likelihood of conventional wars will sharply increase, turning the whole of Europe into some kind of archetypical "Balkans". "No further proliferation" (something that actually happened) seemed to Mearsheimer as the most plausible outcome, though not the safest, since Germany would feel threatened and would choose to go nuclear while at the same time bullying smaller and weaker central European powers. The most likely scenario according to Mearsheimer is further nuclear proliferation in Europe (which actually did not happen) with preventative attacks and mismanagement of missiles being the greatest possible among the perils foreseen. Fortunately for all of us, none of Mearsheimer's lackadaisical predictions came true and Europe did not undergo "Balkanization". However, for the sake of this chapter, the most interesting is how Mearsheimer rejects the competing theories. In fact, Mearsheimer only challenges three of the competing antitheses: 1. obsolescence of war, 2. liberalism-pacifism (which he ironically calls peace-loving democracies) and 3. economic liberalism. The latter incorporates both liberal intergovernmentalism and neo-functionalism. The essence of the "obsolescence of war" argument rests on the thought that modern-day wars are devastating on an enormous scale and that states will not opt for going to war. Mearsheimer finds this explanation the most convincing, though it may not be sufficiently compelling to exclude the prospect of a *blitzkrieg*. He also highlighted that the dreadfulness of WWI did not prevent WWII.

Liberalism is not a homogeneous paradigm. Both neo-functionalism and liberal intergovernmentalism are branches of a political direction called "liberalism". Liberalism professes the belief in representative democracy and the market system which may have a contradictory relationship, as the one person/one vote principle in the polity does not translate into equality in the market place. Therefore, a distinction between political liberals and market liberals is justified to which one could add social liberals who have a permissive attitude towards different social values and practices. Social liberalism accepts the notion of the welfare state, usually supported by social democrats, provided that the state does not become too dominant. A distinction has also been drawn between evolutionary liberalism (Immanuel Kant) and revolutionary liberalism (Thomas Paine), both working in the late 18th century. The former approach accepts competing preferences between actors that make cooperation more difficult, while the latter believes in ultimate harmony and consensus. In any case, belief in the possibility of social progress is typical of liberalism. The society tends to move towards higher levels of development and freedom which would be accompanied by the spread of democracy and benign capitalism (Väyrynen 2011).

Neo-functionalism, the brainchild of Ernst Haas, is an eclectic approach based on Mitrany's functionalism and Monnet's pragmatic view towards furthering European integration. Interestingly, Haas has never considered his brainchild a theory and later just abandoned it after realizing that his not only descriptive and explanatory, but also rather prescriptive approach is not on par with reality (Schmitter 2005, 255-256). Nevertheless, it is still believed that neo-functionalism firmly entrenched its place in the family of IR theories (Rosamond 2005, 19). In fact, neo-functionalism is probably the most frequently criticized theory. Nevertheless, not all its merits were utterly annihilated.

The central message of neo-functionalists is the following: "despite states remaining relevant actors in furthering integration, self-interested regional bureaucrats of the resourceful international secretariats are keen to exploit inevitable spillover effects" (Schmitter 2003, 16). A closer look to Schmitter's arguments reveals that by "international secretariats" he primarily meant the supranational institutions of the EU. As for the "self-interested bureaucrats" argument it was widely used to explain the persistence of international organizations, including but not limited to the military alliances. Stephen Walt, for example, argued that "alliance generates a large formal bureaucracy, this will create a cadre of individuals whose professional perspectives and career prospects are closely tied to maintaining the relationship. Such individuals are likely to view the alliance as intrinsically desirable and will be reluctant to abandon it even when circumstances change" (Walt 2008, 166). At the same time, exploiting spillover effects requires power (even limited), vested in supranational agents that gives them some autonomy. It is argued that the institutions themselves consciously create situations that can be tackled only through spillover (Rosamond 2005, 11). Another prerequisite is democracy "reigning" in the member states (Schmitter 2005, 257). Neo-functionalists distinguish three types of spillover: functional, political and cultivated (Tranholm-Mikkelsen 1991, 10). Functional spillover refers to the technical necessity to concentrate more power in the hands of the central regional bodies and in fact reflects the most banal general understanding of neo-functionalist, i.e. integration in one sphere triggers integration in another spheres. For example, monetary policy delegated to the European Central Bank required strict and stiff fiscal policy coordination among EU-19. Political spillover is about the wish of different domestic stakeholders of member states to seek supranational rather than national solutions as the former are less susceptible for frequent changes. This process was later labelled "engrenage". And finally, cultural spillover refers to the ability of central regional organs (secretariats) to promote a pro-integration culture by elevating common interest of the member states. Haas argued that without the impartial mediation and arbitrage of supranational bodies, member states stick to "the minimum common denominator determined by the least cooperative partner" (Tranholm-Mikkelsen 1991, 6).

Neo-functionalist arguments are predicated upon the following assumptions:

1. States are no longer the predominant actors in the regional system.

2. The integration process is interest-driven rather than identity-driven.
3. Decisions about integration are happening under the conditions of asymmetric information and knowledge.
4. Functions and issue-areas are the locomotives of further integration.
5. Regional/international bureaucrats are interested in furthering the integration process. This argument is completely in line with one of the realist arguments (Walt, 1997, 166) explaining the persistence of military alliances (the role of NATO bureaucracy in keeping the alliance alive).
6. Integration occurs not as a result of identical, but convergent and overlapping interests of the agents.
7. Integration is not confined to the initial treaty signed, but is a dynamic process revolved around new agreements (Schmitter, 2005, 259).

To these assumptions we would add two more: neo-functionalists disregard the possibility of use of force in case of an unpleasant outcome of negotiation. Such assumption is intrinsic to all those schools originating from liberal political thought. Secondly, neo-functionalists assume that the timing of the integration process is not set or in other words they do not specify when and under which conditions spillover effects will stop.

The relevant literature is full of criticism of neo-functionalism. This criticism may be summarized in the following way:

1. Neo-functionalism is silent about widening of the EU, i.e. EU enlargement. In fact, Schmitter posits that neo-functionalists might respond by arguing that the new member states already accept the EU *acquis* in the negotiation process and by the virtue of being EU members they are *ipso facto* members of all the EU institutions (Schmitter 2005, 259).
2. Neo-functionalism does not differentiate between high and low politics. In fact, states will relatively easily concede sovereignty over the issues of low politics (such as trade) than high politics (such as foreign and security policy).

3. Neo-functionalism does not duly acknowledge the power and pro-integration efforts of other institutions, namely the Court of Justice of the European Union (CJEU) and the Parliament, as it is excessively focused on the role of the "supranational secretariat". Such critiques, though pertinent, are a bit unfair, since only "integration through law" theory pays a close attention to the role of the CJEU, while Moravcsik, for instance, earlier found its role unique and later attempted to explain it so that it does not contradict the pivotal doctrine of his theory (will be discussed below).
4. Neo-functionalism fails to address the impact of exogenous factors, i.e. trends and developments happening outside Europe which may both strengthen and weaken the European integration. In fact, neo-functionalism tackled this criticism by arguing that the spillover effect is not automatic, but crisis-driven. Therefore, as a result of crisis not only spillover, but also spillback is completely possible. This is particularly important against the background of European external action. For example, the 1999 Partnership and Cooperation Agreement (PCA) with Armenia and deeper cooperation within the Comprehensive and Enhanced Partnership Agreement (CEPA) can be ascribed to the neo-functionalist logic of argumentation on cooperation in many fields resulting from the cooperation in one field. However, stepping back from the Association Agreement (AA) to CEPA is in contrast to neo-functionalist maxims and is more in line with the spillback argument of neo-functionalism.

Liberal intergovernmentalism is another branch of a much broader liberal school of IR, premised on the following two core assumptions: 1. International law and agreements are coupled with international institutions like the UN that allow the pooling of resources for common goals, 2. The spread of capitalism through international organizations established market-based economies all over the world and makes any potential conflict unreasonable (Meiser 2017, 24). Moravcsik argued that European integration is a brilliant example of an intergovernmental regime that manages economic interdependence through negotiated policy coordination (Moravcsik 1993, 474). If one is to single out the key three concepts of his theory those would be (1) rational behavior of states, (2) national preferences and (3) interstate negotiation. The central message of his theory is that the European agenda is shaped primarily in the national capitals and afterwards negotiated in Brussels through intergovernmental negotiations. Juxtaposing this with the graph demonstrating the interaction between supply and demand which is well-known from the classical economics, he stated that the domestic sector represents the demand side of the curve, while the international bargain—the supply side (Moravcsik 1993, 482). He further elaborates that national governments are not necessarily keen to engage in economic cooperation or policy coordination through supranational entities. In fact, they do it for two major purposes: 1. to satisfy the domestic constituencies and preserve power in the democratic system, 2. to use international agreements for the sake of economic growth and efficiency through pushing domestic producers towards necessary adjustments under the pretence of "Brussels" (Moravcsik 1993, 485-486). This is how he interprets the acquiescence of nationalists like Churchill and de Gaulle with the partial relinquishment of sovereignty. However, domestic constituencies are not necessarily made up of exporters pushing for freer trade, while importers would oppose such a policy. Nonetheless, market liberalization occurs when "adjustment is relatively costless or compensation between winners and losers can be arranged, distributional effects need not create opposition to free trade." In addition, Moravcsik believes that producers are more organized and keener to advance their interests as they have a higher per capita benefit/loss as a result of policy changes that outweigh the costs of organizing, monitoring and representing the concentrated groups (Moravcsik 1993, 488).

The argument of intergovernmental bargains is premised on the following assertions: 1. governments cooperate under the absence of military threat or coercion (these assumptions, as we mentioned above, are common in all liberal theories), 2. transaction costs of intergovernmental negotiations are low as negotiations take place over protracted time periods (Moravcsik 1993, 489). Furthermore, it is assumed that the more alternatives the governments have the less interested they are in the outcome; however, they try their best not to be insulated and excluded (Moravcsik 1993, 499). Due to time limitations governments tend to do logrolling and issue linkages. The latter is basically about compromise, i.e. you accept my offer, I will accept yours. The classical example is German acquiescence with CAP price in order to get access to French industrial markets (Moravcsik 1993, 506). The raison d'être of supranational bodies according to Moravcsik is dualistic: 1. to diminish the threat of non-compliance by the partners, 2. to "sell" the policies to domestic constituencies.

Liberal intergovernmentalism was criticized on both ontological and epistemological grounds (Moravcsik 1995, 613; Schimmelfennig 2003, 81). It is considered not a theory, but an approach. As Moravcsik truly pointed out, some of the assumptions of liberal intergovernmentalism are anchored in well-known theories, namely the theory of rational actors and theory of bargaining. As for epistemological criticism, Moravcsik responds that the criticism is unreasonably strict and by that very token all mid-range theories of IR, i.e. a considerable part of the classics of IR literature, shall be rejected (Moravcsik 1995, 613).

The core assumptions of liberal intergovernmentalism were also challenged by historical-institutionalists. They argue that liberal intergovernmentalism might be applicable to European external relations only in their initial stages. In particular, historical institutionalists argue that the institutionalization of habits and patterns in the domain of foreign and security policy are so well entrenched in intergovernmentalist configuration, that this hampers any graduation to supranational decision-making (Krotz and Maher 2011, 561-562). Therefore, institutionalism is not only a catalyst of, but equally a constraint to integration (Hodson and Peterson 2017, 19). However, once the institutions are established, it becomes very difficult to roll the trajectory of institutional development back even if the changed preferences of the member states do not meet the existing institutional structure. They argue that institutions strive hard to sustain themselves (Schimmelfennig 2003, 82). Against this background, the Western European Union (WEU), a European organization with military purposes, may serve as an example. Since its establishment in 1954, WEU was only called upon once during the war in Bosnia (Dinan 2010, 119-120) and it finally ceased its functioning in 2011. The criticism of historical-institutionalism, though relevant, does not undermine the value of liberal intergovernmentalism significantly. In fact, Moravcsik may argue that with each treaty amendment member states try to match the institutional architecture to their essential needs.

However, the most important criticism of liberal intergovernmentalism that targets its roots is the case bias. It is argued that Moravcsik deliberately focuses on cases requiring unanimity of the member states and ignores the pro-integration initiatives of the EU Commission and the CJEU (Schimmelfennig 2003, 82). Furthermore, Moravcsik does not take into account the socialization effect of the governmental officials when the latter meet in different configurations (Council of Ministers, COREPER, etc.). In addition, though admitting that liberal intergovernmentalism is not about day-to-day policy of the EU, Moravcsik does not specify how the strongest domestic groups, like unions of producers, try to limit the power of the EU Commission to avoid decisions like "Europe free of roaming fee". One cannot disregard the fact that with each treaty amendment, supranational institutions like the EU Commission and the CJEU, as well as the transnational Parliament, found themselves in a stronger position vis-à-vis the member states.

Overall, neo-functionalism and liberal intergovernmentalism, though sharing the same philosophical roots, are in disagreement about the "drivers" of European integration. Liberal intergovernmentalism, however, seems to be less permeable and not (yet) abandoned by its creator Andrew Moravcsik. The major reason is that liberal intergovernmentalism, unlike neo-functionalism, is not mono-causal, but tripartite (member state preferences, intergovernmental bargains, supranational institutions as "watchdogs"), thus taking into consideration more relevant factors.

Realism rejected both liberal intergovernmentalism and neo-functionalism with the argument that the primary aim of states is not prosperity, but security (Mearsheimer 1990, 43). He further argues that states care more about relative gains (who gets more) than absolute ones. He also believed that economic interdependence, instead of strengthening peace, might actually lead to war as states do not like dependency and will try to get rid of it. As a response from the side of liberals, Moravcsik criticized such an approach, stating that realists and neo-realists treat states as "billiard balls" or "black boxes" with unchangeable preferences, while in reality preferences are defined domestically and remain variable (Moravcsik 1993, 481). Admitting that an uneven distribution of welfare might provoke opposition against policy coordination, Moravcsik (1993, 487) argued that such opposition and unwillingness to cooperate can be overcome by collective action of the governments. As for democratic-peace theory, Mearsheimer acknowledged a correlation between democracy and the absence of war. However, he argues that correlation does not mean causality. He further noted that there is no evidence in history that democracies do not fight each other because democracies are a relatively new way of governance. In particular, he refers to the Fashoda incident between France and Britain in 1898 and the covert warfare orchestrated by democratic USA against democratic Guatemala and Chile (Mearsheimer 1990, 51).

EU external governance theory is yet another "member of the liberal family of EU-intrinsic IR theories". The phrase "European governance" implies defining norms, rules and mechanisms by EU institutions in spheres where EU institutions have (or share) power within the boundaries of the EU. However, since the 1990s scholars have started to study European governance beyond the formal borders of the EU. By external governance we mean "a system of rules that exceeds the volunteerism implicit in terms of cooperation and refers to recurrent forms of coordinated action that aim at the collectively binding agreements" (Lavenex 2011, 374).

For an adequate and exhaustive understanding of the nature of EU external governance, it is of utmost importance to single out its mechanisms, principles, dimensions, geographic scope as well as the "carrots" the third countries are expecting to obtain once successfully domesticizing the peculiarities of EU internal governance. Schimmelfennig classifies the mechanisms of EU external governance into two clusters: direct and indirect. The former implies the direct involvement of the EU in the Europeanization of third countries either through stipulating conditions (conditionality) or through persuading the latter of the righteousness of the rules and norms applicable in the EU (socialization). While the latter implies third countries' voluntary Europeanization either based on cost-benefit calculations (externalization) or based on the resonance of EU rules and policies (imitation).

EU external governance theory is predicated upon the following major principles:

1. Fostering regional economic integration and promoting the idea of establishment of supranational organizations mirroring the EU.
2. Spurring the creation of transnational markets, viz. propagating a neoliberal economic model (model intrinsic to EU).
3. Promoting democracy and fundamental human rights and freedoms (as norm entrenched in all EU states' constitutions).

The EU external governance is implemented in the following two dimensions: regulatory boundary and organizational boundary. Regulatory boundary demonstrates the extent to which the regulatory extension is accompanied by organizational inclusion, i.e., the possibilities for third countries to participate in the determination of the relevant *acquis* (Lavenex 2011, 373).

According to Schimmelfennig, geography matters strongly. The further we move away from the EU, the more indirect and weaker its impact becomes. Its direct neighbors (the quasi-member states and candidates for membership) experience the most direct and strongest Europeanization, whereas the more distant world or far away regions are only subject to indirect, patchy or weak Europeanization (Schimmelfennig 2010, 18). In other words, the farther the third countries are geographically located the less they are affected by EU regulations. For a comprehensive illustration of the EU impact on different countries and regions, Schimmelfennig proposes the following table:

Table 1: External governance according to countries (Schimmelfennig 2010)

Country	Mechanism	Conditions	Impact
Quasi-members:	Conditionality and externalization	Strong dependence	Strong, partial
Candidate countries	Conditionality	Strong dependence and a strong incentive	Strong, general
Neighborhood countries	Conditionality and socialization	Medium dependence, weak incentives	Medium, partial
Other	Imitation and socialization	Weak interdependence	Weak

To boost its external governance the EU suggests "carrots" to the partners eager to adopt its rules and norms and to adhere to its values. The EU's large and attractive market serves as a leverage to impact on most of its partners. At the same time, for the candidates and potential candidates one more privilege is offered—the possibility of EU accession. The Union also relies on the EU Commission's and member states' external aid programs. In addition, along with the "carrots" the EU might also apply "the stick", i.e. sanctions applied against those breaching, for instance, its main values. Overall, in the spheres where the EU Commission has exclusive rights (like foreign trade) the efficacy of EU external governance is much higher compared to the spheres not covered by the EU *acquis*, or where the possible unanimous approach is thwarted because of discrepancies between member states. Furthermore, the EU external governance has sometimes unsuccessful outcomes conditioned by counter-steps of its regional rivals, such as Russia.

It is hard to make a dialogue between EU external governance theory and the other aforesaid liberal theories as the former is concerned with explaining the EU external action policy and the successes and limits thereof, while the latter are more focused on the integration processes. Nevertheless, it is more in line with the realist way of thinking than the other discussed liberal theories. Indeed, the core argument of EU external governance theory—the more the partner country hinges on the EU economy the more power the EU can exercise with regard to it, fully fits with the aforesaid second principle of Realism defined by Morgenthau. However, unlike most liberal theories and liberal intergovernmentalism in particular, realists paid little attention to domestic considerations of the member states in an attempt to explain the external action policy of the EU. This is astounding since realists believe that international system shapes the security environment in which states operate, structure alone does not determine the outcome (Krotz and Maher 2011, 560). The problem is that realists challenge something that in fact exists—the ever-closer union which becomes more and more tightly knit with each and every treaty change. At the same time, however, being EU-centered and EU-focused EU external governance theory does not duly consider geopolitical competition, i.e., the limits of the EU's ability to exercise its power against the background of geopolitical rivalry with other major regional powers. In other words, it does not explain the ability of the EU to pursue its interests in the partner countries once the latter are at odds with the interests of other major powers/geopolitical rivals (e.g., Russia or China) which also have a considerable interest in the partner country.

Constructivism is a grand IR theory along with realism and liberalism. Constructivism sees the world as socially constructed. It is ontologically agnostic, i.e., it does not include or exclude any variable as meaningful and views the changes occurring in the world as a result of changing practices in the intersubjective world order (Hopf 1998). As Wendt stated, 500 nuclear weapons are far less threatening to the USA than the dinky nuclear arsenal of North Korea (Theys 2017, 36).

The understanding of identities is of paramount importance against the backdrop of European integration. Concepts like "United States of Europe", "Federal Europe" and "one single European citizenship" are disputed mostly on ideational grounds by sceptics and pessimists. In reality, however, as Risse pointed out, it is wrong to conceptualize European identity in zero-sum terms (Risse 2003, 166). Risse claims that identities may relate to each other in three ways. The first is about the nested identities similar to the Russian doll Matryoska, i.e., one identity inside the other. The core (the smallest doll) is the identity one associates himself the most. For instance, Risse mentioned that reports about EU Commission officials suggest that Europe is at the core of their identity, while the national identity is in the periphery. This might be explained by the fact that unlike other citizens, for the officials working in the EU Commission Europe and the EU are not something remote and intangible (Risse 2003, 166-168). Identities might also be cross-cutting. For instance, one may have a very strong gender identity and weaker European identity. As Hooghe mentioned, Eurosceptic attitude depends on whether a person is exclusively or inclusively conceiving his or her national identity, since individuals with an exclusive national identity are more prone to Euroscepticism (Hooghe and Rauh 2017, 13). And finally, the third way to conceptualize identity is to say that multiple identities are inseparable from each other (Risse 2003, 168). It is believed that EU membership significantly strengthened the European identity.

Furthermore, "Europe" is more and more equated with "the EU". For instance, when Italy, one of the founding members of the EU, was about to enter the euro-zone, the slogan was "entrare l'Europa (entering Europe)" (Risse 2003, 169). In addition, constructivists agree that identities, though slowly, can change.

Both liberal intergovernmentalism (Moravcsik) and social-constructivism state that ideas / ideologies do matter. The disagreement is about how they matter and to what extent. For Moravcsik ideas are just a mask, a cover to justify the rationally-motivated actions of the agents. Agents use ideas to "nicely package" their interest-driven positions. For constructivists, however, identities as mentioned above are the key drivers behind every action. There is even a conviction in social science literature that war is an outcome of misperception (Jervis 1988). Moravcsik appreciated Checkel for his empirical study, saying that the latter managed to bring constructivism out of its metatheoretical clouds. Nevertheless, he challenges Checkel on methodological grounds. Particularly, he argues that the above-mentioned four hypotheses are not intrinsic only to constructivism (Moravcsik 2001, 228). He offers alternative rationalist hypotheses. Overall, the central message of Moravcsik is that it is difficult to figure out whether socialization happens as a result of rationalist considerations (like coercion, manipulation) or social-constructivist considerations (like persuasion). He accuses Checkel for not being able to produce distinctively social-constructivist hypotheses (Moravcsik 2001, 233-236).

Checkel argues (1999, 548) that his methodology and hypotheses are strictly interconnected, i.e., through his methods he is able to check the impact of persuasion on preference change, thus effectively controlling the impact of other possible intervening variables. Furthermore, he argues that Moravcsik brought up counterarguments against arguments never stated by him. Checkel (1999, 548) argues that he "did not equate rational choice with the realist notion of coercion, but with manipulation and strategic usage of language." In fact, a close reading of Checkel's arguments reveals that the claims of Moravcsik are manipulations and attempts of building a "straw man".

Constructivism has one, yet unsurmountable flaw—it very well explains what happened but does not predict the future. Hence, it cannot be applied to understand future integration/disintegration of the

EU. It is wrong to compare theories like neo-functionalism to constructivism as the former is prescriptive. In contrast, constructivism is only an interpretative theory as it does not foretell how and towards which direction the socially constructed reality will be changed. Last but not least, the major constructivist theories have paid little attention to European integration. In 1999, however, a special issue of the Journal of European Public Policy was devoted to constructivism and European integration (Moravcsik 2001, 226). In that issue, constructivists stressed the impact of intersubjectivity and social context on European integration which was regarded as a continuing process (Christiansen et al. 1999, 528). In particular, it was argued that intersubjectivity and social context are the clues to grasp the reasons behind reaching the current stage of European integration; putting it aside would mean missing a focal part of the entire process (Christiansen et al. 1999, 529).

Armenia as the Leading Case

EU external action policies vis-à-vis the three republics of the South Caucasus are not homogeneous. Both the extent and the intensity of the cooperation is variable. Out of the three, Georgia has the closest relationship with the EU: although the EU recently postponed to grant Georgia the status of a candidate for membership, it granted the "perspective" of EU membership; i.e., Georgia will be offered the status of a candidate country once it is ready from the viewpoint of the EU (EU Commission 2022).

Armenia's case is particularly noteworthy as it reflects an attempt to pursue a complementary foreign policy. Prior to signing CEPA with the EU in 2017, Armenia was considered to be firmly under Russia's influence. This was evidenced by Armenia's decision to join the EAEU in 2015, a Russian-led economic bloc that also includes Belarus, Kazakhstan, and Kyrgyzstan. Armenia's decision to sign CEPA with the EU demonstrated the EU's ability to engage with a country that was previously seen as being within Russia's sphere of influence. In contrast, Georgia has been actively seeking closer relations with the EU for many years and has already signed an AA with the EU in 2014. In the case of Georgia, it is the AA which is indicative of the desire to both widen and deepen cooperation with the EU. Armenia, by comparison, was also offered an AA. But after it was initialled, Armenia refused to sign it and made a U-turn by joining the Russian-led EAEU. The AA was then superseded by CEPA which in essence is "everything minus political integration" with the EU. Compared to the earlier PCA, CEPA most importantly deals with the approximation of Armenian legislation to the *acquis communautaire*. It does not touch on issues of "high politics", such as the security of Armenia's nuclear power plant or ratification of the Rome Statute of the International Criminal Court. Therefore, it can be concluded Georgia's case does not demonstrate the same kind complementarity in conducting foreign policy. Similarly, Azerbaijan has not shown a willingness to engage with the EU to the same extent as Armenia. While Azerbaijan has been a participant in the EU's Eastern Partnership program, it has not shown an interest in signing an AA with the EU or pursuing closer political ties. In fact, Azerbaijan pursued closer ties with Turkey and Russia rather than the EU.

To summarize the main events, following a meeting with Russian Foreign Minister Sergey Lavrov in 2012, Armenia's then Prime-Minister Tigran Sargsyan announced that accession to the Customs Union (as the precursor to the EAEU) is neither expedient nor beneficial from an economic viewpoint, particularly due to inflation-related risks. Instead, he expressed the commitment of Armenia to comply with European standards and to sign a free trade agreement with the EU.[i] Even one year later, during a joint press conference with Polish President Bronislaw Komorowksi, President Serzh Sargsyan declared that "Armenians are the nation which is a carrier of European values and our goal is to advance our society based on those very values".[ii] Notwithstanding the previous declarations, after three months, during a joint press conference with President Vladimir Putin, President Sargsyan noted that Armenia and Russia are in one security structure and that it is unfeasible and inefficient to stay away from the relevant geopolitical area. Moreover, he asserted that Armenia and the members of the Customs Union are intertwined with "a thousand threads".

Overall, there is a vivid contradiction between the declarations of Armenia's ex-Prime Minister (who is a member of the President's party) and the President of Armenia.

To gain a deeper comprehension of why Armenia chose to join the EAEU, content analysis was performed on President Serzh Sargsyan's speeches and interviews regarding the topic that was available in the official website of the President of Armenia. The analysis focused on the speeches and interviews of the President because he held the highest position of power in the country and was constitutionally responsible for conducting foreign policy at the time. This analysis aimed to identify the underlying factors that influenced Armenia's decision. Overall, six speeches and interviews given by President Sargsyan between 2012 and 2015 were analyzed. Based on the transcripts of the text and interviews, five comprehensive codes were developed to capture the theme in a way that avoids redundancy and ensures each code is distinct from the others. Once the data was coded, the frequency of each and every code was calculated based on the number of times it appears in the text. This method is also known as "frequency analysis". The mean was calculated by adding up the total frequency counts for each code and divide by the total number of units of analysis (six transcripts).

The table below shows the key concepts which according to President Sargsyan were critical behind Armenia's U-turn.

Table 2. Political factors behind Armenia's joining the EAEU according to President Serzh Sargsyan

Descriptor	Frequency	Mean
Coercion	3	0.5
Strategic partnership, CSTO	6	1
Choice of civilisation	2	0.33
Gas	5	0.83

The first descriptor, i.e., coercion, indicates that according to President Sargsyan Russia did not coerce Armenian authorities to make a U-turn and join the EAEU. Moreover, in his press conference dated 18 March 2013, he even noted that Russian officials were not interested to see Armenia in the EAEU, but that Armenia was following its own interests.[iii] The second descriptor implies that President Sargsyan often referred to a strategic partnership with Russia to explicate and justify his decision to join the EAEU. The third descriptor implies that President Sargsyan denied that the choice of Armenia is a civilizational choice. The meaning of the third descriptor is best illustrated in the following direct quotation from President Sargsyan's speech delivered at the Embassy of Armenia to the Czech Republic on 29 September 2014:

> "Our choice is not a choice of a civilization. It's a choice that emanates from the interests of our people. We can't sign free trade agreement and appreciate gas and electricity three-fold. If it turns out that the brandy doesn't appropriate with European standards, then we'll cease growing grapes. Do you want this? Suppose you do a manifestation with five people what do you want to reach? Should you decide how we need to live?" (Aravot Daily 2013).

All in all, there are a number of proofs both in official documents and in the officials' speeches and interviews to argue that energy interests were pivotal factors behind Armenia's integration into the EAEU. By contrast, there is not enough evidence to assert that security played a critical role in Armenia's accession decision. Furthermore, EAEU accession failed to coerce Azerbaijan to decrease the frequency of armistice violation.

The EU has agreed to Armenia's decision to choose the Russia-led EAEU over the AA with the EU. The unique security circumstances which were further exacerbated after the recent forty-four days war in Artsakh (aka Nagorno-Karabakh), the energy dependence on Russia, the presence of a huge Armenian diaspora in Russia as a tool in the hands of the Kremlin, and last but not least the paramount role of Russia in key sectors of the Armenian economy were duly accounted for and motivated the political leadership of Armenia to perform its U-turn. Most of these factors underlie the above-analysed speech of President Sargsyan. Still, it was argued that Armenia made its choice "under the gun" (Grigoryan 2014).

Inter-paradigm Dialogue in the Case of Armenia

Realism

Despite realism's emphasis on states' desire for self-aggrandizing, the EU did little to vie for its power in the South Caucasus with its geopolitical rival Russia. The former Foreign Minister of Armenia claimed that EU officials were pushing Armenia to choose between the EAEU and the EU (Radio Liberty 2015). The perks offered by the EU such as preferential access to the European market through the GSP+ mechanism or grants to both public sector and civil society organizations apparently did not hold up to the geopolitical reality Armenia was facing. Furthermore, as the EU consists of very diverse internal constituencies, it lacks the ability to carry out a homogeneous external action policy as compared to any individual member state, let alone Russia. External action is still mostly in the domain of national governments.

The case shows that realism is most limited in explaining the EU external action policy's effectiveness in the case of Armenia since the EU is neither able nor willing to use hard power simply because it lacks it. Unlike the other domains where the EU Commission has either exclusive or shared competences, the member states' potency in the domain of foreign and security policy is largely unfettered. Realism, on the other hand, will probably help to understand Armenia's U-turn from the EU to the EAEU given the security challenges faced by the country and energy dependence on Russia. In other words, realism is of a great help to explain the foreign policy of Armenia, however it is of a little help to explain the EU external action policy with regard to Armenia as the EU, unlike its geopolitical rivals, is an economic power having just soft power in its arsenal.

Neo-functionalism and Liberal Intergovernmentalism

Can liberal intergovernmentalism and neo-functionalism explain the EU's external action vis-à-vis Armenia? By critically examining the arguments of the neo-functionalists, one may deduce that they are to a very limited extent transferrable to the domain of external action and may offer only limited explanatory potential. For example, one may juxtapose the PCA between the EU and Armenia with the spillover effect described and referred to by the neo-functionalists, arguing that out of cooperation with the neighbor/partner country (Armenia in this case) in domain X a need for deeper cooperation in domain Y emerged and also cooperation in domains Y and Z, thus necessitating supersession of the PCA by a more exhaustive CEPA. Indeed, one may argue that creating a level playing field in terms of granting no less favorable treatment to Armenian companies than that accorded to any third country for the establishment of Armenian companies in the

EU as stipulated in the Article 23 PCA necessitated the signature of the Common Aviation Agreement between the parties in 2021, since the air transport was among the exemptions from the rule. However, such neo-functionalist approach cannot be consistently applicable as it would be unable to explain the backstep from signing the AA to CEPA which resulted in a lesser extent of cooperation. Nevertheless, the central role of the secretariat, i.e., the EU Commission, is also difficult to overlook as it is the main driver of the negotiations from the European side. However, one has to mention that even the developers of the theory did not extend it to foreign policy, but restricted it to the explication of integration process only. Hence, neo-functionalism has a limited explanatory power to explicate the EU's external action policy. On the other hand, it is worthwhile to examine different sub-branches of liberalism in combination and to contrast them with one another in order to better understand the weaker points of each theory.

Admittedly, liberal intergovernmentalism better explains the EU's external action. Member states are driven by the interests of the private sector to use EU institutions both as instruments to advance their policy goals and as watchdogs for overseeing the commitments. CEPA may serve as a good example. The bulk of the legal document is about the approximation of Armenian legislation with the EU *acquis communautaire*. It meets the interest of EU exporters who do not need to produce goods in standards other than the EU's own standards to have them exported to the Armenian market. The EU established a Partnership Committee with Armenia to diminish the possibility of non-compliance by the latter.

A good example is the section of CEPA dealing with cognac and champagne. France, for example, used the bargaining power of the EU to advance its national economic interests. Article 235.5 CEPA states the following:

> "By way of derogation from paragraph 4, prior trademarks of the Republic of Armenia which consist of or contain the geographical indication of the European Union 'Cognac' or 'Champagne', including in transcription or translation, registered for like products and not complying with the relevant specification, shall be invalidated, revoked or modified in order to eliminate that name as an element of the whole trademark, at the latest within 14 years for 'Cognac' and two years for 'Champagne', following the entry into force of this Agreement."[iv]

Obviously, this clause is in line with French economic interests, as both Cognac and Champagne are geographic areas in France known for their beverage brands. On the other hand, Article 237.4 CEPA, which is about the financial and technical assistance to Armenia as a compensation for the loss of competitiveness due to succumbing to EU (French) demands regarding renouncing the usage of "cognac" and "champagne" brands, clearly demonstrates the compromising wording reached as a result of the active bargaining of the Armenian side. The Partnership Committee is called upon to monitor the implementation of the Agreement, i.e., it is the watchdog. The lack of desire to vie for Armenia with Russia or to offer something more to Georgia may also be explained through the application of the "economic interests of the members" argument (Moravcsik 1993, 490) underlying liberal intergovernmentalism. Indeed, being a bigger and geographically closer market to the EU. Georgia is a more attractive and important partner for the latter than Armenia. The same can be said about Moldova. One may object that by the same token liberal intergovernmentalism will not be able to explicate the murky relationship between the EU and Belarus, for example, which much bigger, closer and much more important partner for the EU than Armenia can ever be. However, such objections and comparisons are intrinsically erroneous as Belarus unlike Georgia, Armenia and Moldova was not eager to deepen and develop the cooperation with the EU. Neither did it aspire to sign an AA with the latter and as of June 2021 it suspended its participation in the EaP. Overall, liberal intergovernmentalism may be applied for both understanding and explaining the EU's external action at least in cases when there is a reciprocal aspiration to deepen and develop the cooperation, despite the fact that it was initially developed to explain European integration. On the example of the EU-Armenia relationship, it is clear that the theory is well-suited to finely explain the EU's external action policy.

EU External Governance Theory

CEPA is quite a fine "laboratory" to test EU external governance theory. CEPA is mostly about the harmonization of policies and the approximation of Armenian legislation with the EU *acquis*. One may find the term "approximation" 40 times in the Agreement. Therefore, one has solid grounds to argue that "socialization" is truly present. As for conditionality, visa policies stipulated by the EU are a salient example. As it is widely known, reciprocity is a principle that states stick to while implementing their foreign policy. It is perceived as both a tool to solidify the sovereignty and a proof of demonstrating one's commitment to preserve the sovereignty and the attributes thereof. This is not the case when it comes to EU-Armenia visa policies. EU citizens are free to come Armenia while Armenians need visa which might be lifted provided that "conditions for well-managed and secure mobility are in place" (Article 15 CEPA). The presence of conditionality is very noticeable in case of Armenia's foreign policy U-turn from the AA initialled with the EU to joining the EAEU. Reportedly, EU officials pressed Armenia to choose between deeper integration with Europe or with Russia (Radio Liberty 2015). In other words, the Union set a condition for deeper cooperation with Armenia which was not entering the Russia-led EAEU. A mention must be made, however, that such conditionality was more than objective. The EAEU is at the second stage of economic integration, i.e., a customs union when two or more states jointly make trade policy decision such as setting a common tariff for third states or delegate it to supranational bodies. Under such circumstances no individual state can conclude a free trade agreement with another state or a block without the consent of its partners. The AA with the EU implied a free trade agreement between Armenia and the EU, which was truly incompatible with the membership in the EAEU.

However, EU external governance theory is not as strong as liberal intergovernmentalism. For example, it is unsuitable to explain the above-described foreign policy U-turn of Armenia and more importantly the acquiescence of the EU to such a U-turn which might be perceived as harmful to the international prestige of the EU. Furthermore, in the case of Armenia, the regulatory extension of EU rules explained above is quite weak. It is solely confined to the approximation of Armenian legislation with the laws of the EU. Similarly, the inclusion of Armenia in the institutional architecture of the EU is negligible, as it is confined merely to the functioning of bilateral committees and cooperation with a few EU agencies. Overall, EU external governance theory is well suited to explain the day-to-day foreign policy of the EU which was well demonstrated on the example of the EU-Armenia relations. However, it is probably not the best instrument to unearth the motives and considerations of the EU while conducting its external action policy.

Social Constructivism

Applying constructivism to the explanation of EU external action is a challenging task. It might be tempting to argue that the identity-driven politicians of Europe have no plans to move closer to Armenia due to the perception of Armenians as "the others". However, it might be extremely difficult to accept or reject such hypotheses predicating merely on documents. In other words, unlike liberal intergovernmentalism or EU external governance theory such statement is unlikely to find any support or opposition in the PCA or CEPA. In fact, constructivism and EU external action are very broad topics that require primary data-based analysis (e.g., interviews with the negotiators, focus group discussions and so on). On the other hand, constructivism, being an "umbrella" theory, may not only be suitable for the explanation of nearly each and every phenomenon in IR, but also complementary to the other theories. For instance, the tenets of constructivism may be helpful to solidify the EU-intrinsic EU external governance theory. One may argue that the EU wishes others to mirror its own identity, therefore it exports its norms and value through various tools such as conditionality, socialization, externalization and imitation. In such a way the EU external governance theory is being subjugated to constructivism. However, by the same token the (neo)realists would argue that through conditionality, socialization, externalization and imitation the EU wishes to export security lest it imports insecurity! Beyond any doubt identity is an important variable to be considered while analyzing the foreign policy of a state or an entity like the EU. However, the extent to which it should account for the outcome of the foreign policy is debatable and requires meticulous examination of each case and therefore might be varied from case to case.

Conclusion

European external action is a new and unique phenomenon, both for the world and the social sciences. Each of the aforementioned theories aim to discuss European integration based on their well-known maxims, such as institutions matter, social world is socially constructed or that everything is about power and security. As it is shown above, each of them has merits of its own. Theories like realism and neo-neofunctionalism lack a thorough picture of EU integration. This comes from the mono-causal explanation of European integration. The foreboding of Mearsheimer and the tendency of the EU to develop a successful and institutionalized foreign and security policy foils any perspective of war on the Old Continent. As for constructivism and social constructivism in particular, it is probably impossible to subjugate interests to identity without a deep and primary data-based study. The analysis above showed that liberal theories including liberal intergovernmentalism that was initially developed to explain the process of the European integration have the highest explanatory power. Indeed, liberal intergovernmentalism in combination with EU external governance theory may guide us to better understand the considerations of the politicians in charge of EU external action at least in cases when both the EU and the partner state aspire to deepen and develop the cooperation. The progressing cooperation of CEPA with Armenia can also be attributed to the liberal intergovernmentalist approach, which emphasizes the role of national governments in shaping EU policies and decision-making processes. By recognizing the interests and concerns of Armenia as a partner state, the EU was able to negotiate a mutually beneficial agreement that reflects both parties' priorities.

Acknowledgements

The present study was originally submitted under the title "The EU and its Foreign Policy at the Crossroads of the Theories of International Relations". It was developed in the framework of the EU-funded Jean-Monnet Module "EU Politics, Policies and Polity", implemented at Armenian State University of Economics from 2019 to 2022 (611351-EPP-1-2019-1-AMEPPJMO-MODULE).

Bibliography

Agenda.ge. 2021. "Georgian Parliament Speaker Raises EU flag in Front of Parliament After Right-wing Groups Burned One Last Night." https://agenda.ge/en/news/2021/1880.

Aljazeera. 2022. "Thousands Rally in Georgia in Support of EU Membership Bid." https://www.aljazeera.com/news/2022/6/20/thousands-of-georgians-in-tbilisi-demonstrate-for-eu-candidacy.

Aravot Daily. 2013. "Diary for Me and for Everyone". "You are Interesting People, You Came Here and Want to Decide the Fate of Armenia?"], http://www.aravot.am/2014/09/24/499600.

Checkel, Jeffrey T. 1999. "Social Construction and Integration." *Journal of European Public Policy* 6 (4): 545-560.

Checkel, Jeffrey T. 2001. "Constructivism and Integration Theory: Crash Landing or Safe Arrival." *European Union Politics* 2 (2): 240-249.

Christiansen, Thomas, Knud Erik Jorgensen and Antje Wiener. 1999. "The Social Construction of Europe." *Journal of European Public Policy* 6 (4): 528-544.

Dinan, Desmond. 2010. "Ever Closer Union: An Introduction to European Integration. 4. Baskı." Palgrave MacMillan, Hampshire.

European Union Commission, 2022. "European Neighbourhood Policy and Enlargement Negotiations, Steps Towards Joining." https://neighbourhood-enlargement.ec.europa.eu/enlargement-policy/steps-towards-joining_en.

Foreign Policy. 2017. "Europe is still a Superpower." https://foreignpolicy.com/2017/04/13/europe-is-still-a-superpower/.

Grigoryan, Armen. 2014. "Armenia: Joining under the Gun". in The Central Asia-Caucasus Institute4 (ed.), *Putin's Grand Strategy: The Eurasian Union and its Discontents*. Singapore, 98-109.

Hobbes, Thomas. 1651. "Leviathan or the Matter, Forme, & Power of a Common-wealth Ecclesiasticall and Civill." St. Pauls Church-yard, London.

Hodson, Dermon and Peterson John. 2017. "Theorizing EU Institutions: Why They Matter for Politics and International Relations" in D. Hodson and M. Shackleton (eds.). *The Institutions of the European Union*. Oxford University Press, Oxford.

Hooghe, Liesbet, and Gary Marks. 2009. "A Postfunctionalist Theory of European Integration: From Permissive Consensus to Constraining Dissensus." *British Journal of Political Science* 39 (1): 1-23.

Hopf, Ted. 1998. "The Promise of Constructivism in International Relations Theory." *International Security* 23 (1): 171-200.

International Republican Institute. 2017. Poll: Georgians Support EU Membership; Distrust Russia but Favor Dialogue, April 4, https://www.iri.org/resources/poll-georgians-support-eu-membership-distrust-russia-but-favor-dialogue/.

Jervis, Robert. 1988. "War and Misperception." *The Journal of Interdisciplinary History* 18 (4): 675-700.

Koslowski, Rey. 1999. "A Constructivist Approach to Understanding the European Union as a Federal Polity." *Journal of European Public Policy* 6 (4): 561-578.

Krotz Ulrich and Richard Maher. 2011. "International Relations Theory and the Rise of European Foreign and Security Policy". *World Politics* 63 (3): 548-579.

Lavenex, Sandra. 2011. "Concentric Circles of Flexible 'EUropean' integration: A Typology of EU External Governance Relations." *Comparative European Politics* 9 (4): 372-393.

Legislative Herald of Georgia. 1995. Constitution of the Republic of Georgia. https://matsne.gov.ge/en/document/download/30346/36/en/pdf.

Machiavelli, Niccolo. 1513. "The Prince" *Hertfordshire: Wordsworth Editions*, Hertfordshire.

Mearsheimer, John J. 2018. "Back to the Future: Instability in Europe after the Cold War." *National and International Security*, Taylor & Francis, Routledge, Oxfordshire.

Mearsheimer, John. 1990, "Back to the Future: Instability in Europe after the Cold War". *International Security* 15 (1): 5-56.

Moravcsik, Andrew. 1993. "Preferences and Power in the European Community: A Liberal Intergovernmentalist Approach." *Journal of Common Market Studies* 31 (4): 473-524.

Moravcsik, Andrew. 1995. "Liberal Intergovernmentalism and Integration: A Rejoinder." *Journal of Common Market Studies* 33 (4): 611-628.

Moravcsik, Andrew. 2001. "Bringing Constructivist Integration Theory out of the Clouds: Has it Landed Yet." *European Union Politics* 2 (2): 226-240.

Morgenthau, Hans. 1948. "Politics Among Nations: The Struggle for Peace and Power." Knoph, New York.

Peterson, John. 1995. "Decision-making in the European Union: Towards a Framework for Analysis." *Journal of European Public Policy* 2 (1): 69-93.

President of Armenia. 2012. "The Customs Union Has No Meaning For us. Armenian Prime Minister on the Relationship with Russia. http://www.ko mmersant.ru/doc-y/1908052.

President of Armenia. 2013. Statement by President Serzh Sargsyan at the Joint Press Conference with the President of the Republic of Poland Bronisław Komorowski http://www.president.am/en/interviews-and-press-conferences/item/2013/06/25/President-Serzh-Sargsyan-pre ss-conference-with-the-President-of-Poland.

President of Armenia. 2013. "President Serzh Sargsyan Met with the Representatives of the Mass Media". President of the Republic of Armenia. http://www.president.am/en/interviews-and-press-conferences/item /2013/03/18/President-Serzh-Sargsyan-press-conference.

President of Armenia. 2013. "The RA President Serzh Sargsyan's Remarks at the Press Conference on the Results of the Negotiations with the RF President Vladimir Putin." President of the Republic of Armenia, http:// www.president.am/en/interviews-and-press-conferences/item/2013 /09/03/President-Serzh-Sargsyan-press-conference-working-visit-to-Russian-Federation.

Radio Liberty. 2015. "Armenia 'Forced To Choose Between EU, Russia'", https://www.azatutyun.am/a/27079876.html.

Risse, Thomas, 2003. "Social Constructivism and European Integration". In A. Wiener and T. Diez (eds.), *European Integration Theory*, Oxford University Press, Oxford.

Rosamond, Ben. 2005. "The Uniting of Europe and the Foundation of EU Studies: Revisiting the Neo-functionalism of Ernst B. Haas". *Journal of European Public Policy* 12 (2): 1-24.

Sagan, Scott and Kenneth Waltz. 2013. *The Spread of Nuclear Weapons: An Enduring Debate*. WW Norton & Company, New York.

Schimmelfennig, Frank. 2010. "Europeanisation Beyond the Member States." *Journal for Comparative Government and European Policy* 8 (3): 19-339.

Schimmelfennig, Frank. 2003. "Liberal Intergovernmentalism". in A. Wiener and T. Diez (eds.), *European Integration Theory*. Oxford University Press, Oxford.

Schmitter, Philippe. 2005. "Ernst B. Haas and the Legacy of Neo-functionalism". *Journal of European Public Policy* 12 (2): 255-272.

Theys, Sarina. 2017. "Constructivism", in: S. McGlinchey et al. (eds.) *International Relations E-International Relations Publishing*, Bristol, England.

Tranholm-Mikkelsen, Jeppe, 1991. "Neo-functionalism: Obstinate or Obsolete? A Reappraisal in the Light of the New Dynamism of the EC", *Millennium* 20 (1): 1-22.

Väyrynen, Raimo. 2011. "Approaches to the Study of International Relations", unpublished lecture notes.

Walt, Stephen. 1997."Why Alliances Endure or Collapse". *Survival* 39 (1): 156-179.

---

[i] "The Customs Union Has No Meaning For Us. Armenian Prime Minister on the Relationship with Russia". Kommersant of 4 April 2012., http://www.kommersant.ru/doc-y/1908052.

[ii] Statement by President Serzh Sargsyan at the Joint Press Conference with the President of the Republic of Poland Bronisław Komorowski on 25 June 2013, http://www.president.am/en/interviews-and-press-conferences/item/2013/06/25/President-Serzh-Sargsyan-press-conference-with-the-President-of-Poland.

[iii] The official Website of the President of Armenia, "President Serzh Sargsyan Met with the Representatives of the Mass Media". President of the Republic of Armenia. 18 March 2013. http://www.president.am/en/interviews-and-press-conferences/item/2013/03/18/President-Serzh-Sargsyan-press-conference.

[iv] Ministry of Foreign Affairs of the Republic of Armenia, Comprehensive and Enhanced Partnership Agreement between the European Union and the European Atomic Energy Community and their member states, of the one part, and the Republic of Armenia, of the other part, https://www.mfa.am/filemanager/eu/CEPA_ENG_1.pdf.

Colored versus Velvet: Revolutions in Georgia and Armenia

Ruben Elamiryan and Archil Sikharulidze

Abstract

Revolutions are an inherent part of the political process. The recent wave started as a pro-democratic movement in Serbia, quickly moved beyond the post-Soviet space in the early 2000s, spread to the Arab world and reached Armenia in 2018. The South Caucasus as a comparatively small region offers distinctively different types of such revolutions in Georgia and Armenia. Political protests in Tbilisi and Yerevan have had the same initial motives, being focused on fighting corruption, power abuse and other reflections of the "failed state". But the outcomes of the same appraisals were totally different. The Rose Revolution in Georgia led to a significant geopolitical shift whereas the democratic movement in Yerevan turned into a regime change with no such reshuffle at all. Thus, the Georgian case was labeled as "colored", the Armenian one as "velvet". We find that there are a few key determinants for "colored" and "velvet" revolutions on the ground. Particularly, the geopolitical situation worldwide and in the region plays an important role as well as involvement of various external actors in the processes. Georgia's comparatively peaceful regime change and consequent alignment to the Western political system became possible due to a mainly peaceful geopolitical situation, including common understanding of the regime change necessity in Tbilisi between the US and Russia, generally Moscow's weakness on the global political arena and, therefore, inability of the state to contain Washington's intervention into the South Caucasian region. On the contrary, the Armenian case represents a non-involvement scenario with a highly complicated geopolitical situation and the readiness of Russia to protect its national interests.

Keywords: Georgia, Armenia, Geopolitics, Velvet & Colored Revolutions.

Introduction

In the early 2000s the "colored" revolutions in the post-Soviet space (Georgia, 2003; Ukraine, 2004; Kyrgyzstan, 2005) were in the focus of Western-oriented scholars, experts and politicians who hoped that "peaceful" power transitions and better understanding of the phenomenon will lead to a more democratic, stable, and secure world order. Nevertheless, gradual disappointment over the outcomes in combination with the Arab Spring soon overshadowed this topic, leaving it factually under-researched. The issue was raised again thanks to events in Ukraine (2013-14), but has been overshadowed again by its aftermath, including war in the Donbas and Luhansk regions. And only the generally unexpected processes in Armenia which led to the Armenian Velvet revolution (2018) made it obvious that the era of 'revolutions' in the region is not over yet.

From this perspective the chapter analyzes and compares two cases—the Georgian Revolution of Roses and the Armenian Velvet Revolution. The main objectives are to reveal the conceptual differences and similarities between Colored and Velvet revolutions, as well as their impact on shifts in foreign policy dimensions in Georgia and Armenia. Finally, we discuss the transformation of the geopolitical landscape in the South Caucasus which impacted the foreign policy decision-making in Tbilisi and Yerevan after the revolutions.

To reach the declared objectives the chapter starts with an in-depth case study of the Georgian Revolution of Roses. It is followed by a comprehensive analysis of the case study of the Armenian Velvet Revolution. The comparative analysis section brings together the results of the two case studies, answers the main research questions and comes up with the conclusions.

The research aims to demonstrate that both the Georgian Revolution of Roses and Armenian Velvet Revolution represent clear examples of how "peaceful transitions" led, on the one hand, to Tbilisi's detachment from Moscow and the post-Soviet region in general and, on the other hand, to Yerevan's continuing strong devotion to its strategic alliance with the Kremlin. This happened despite initially declared similar motives and incentives. Secondly, a major difference is about political time and geopolitical environment. During the Georgian Revolution of Roses, the West and the US, in particular, were much more engaged in the South Caucasus which tempted Georgia to think that it could counter-balance Russia with them. On the contrary, currently, especially after the so-called Second Artsakh war, it seems that the Western presence in the South Caucasus is declining, whereas Türkiye and Russia are strengthening their positions.

Rose Revolution of Georgia

The Rose Revolution that took place between 3 and 23 November 2003 has not initially been envisioned by its political leaders and internal/external supporters as a historic geopolitical shift from the pragmatically grounded politics of Eduard Shevardnadze to the ideologically heavily influenced pro-American approach of Mikhail Saakashvili (BBC News 2005). The former Soviet high official Shevardnadze was neither pro-Western nor pro-Russian, despite his active contacts and very close relations with Washington, Brussels, and Moscow. Realizing the Kremlin's grip on the region in general and on Georgia, in particular, including involvement to the conflicts in Abkhazia, Tskhinvali, and Nagorno Karabakh, the President of Georgia maintained dialogue with the Kremlin through CIS membership (The Jamestown Foundation 1997). On the other hand, he steadily approached the West by "knocking" at NATO doors (The Jamestown Foundation 2000). But the shattering effect of the Soviet collapse in combination with Shevardnadze's inability and perhaps unwillingness to fight corruption and combat state malfunctioning, turned Georgia into a classical "failed state". The country as well as Georgian society significantly suffered from abuse of power, lack of political culture, violation of human and property rights, weak judiciary and, most importantly, police violence. Finally, it experienced the strongest economic and societal downfall in the post-Soviet space. By the end of the day, a country morally and emotionally devastated by civil war and two separatist military conflicts, found itself at "rock bottom" (The World Bank Group 2012). Tired and exhausted, Georgian society was looking for a new hope, a leader who would lead the nation to prosperity.

Mikhail Saakashvili, a Western-educated former Minister of Justice in Shevardnadze's Government, quickly gained popularity and support. Being elected in 2004 as president, he soon became a new "messiah" (Markozashvili 2014). Despite being a self-proclaimed

Western-oriented government and assuring its allies, especially the administration of George W. Bush, of its intent to put the state on "democratic railways", the main motives for the Rose Revolution success were not geopolitical (Mitchell 2009; MacFarlane 2011; Kandelaki 2006). Obviously, the youth movement "Kmara" (Companjen et al. 2008) which had played an important role in fighting Shevardnadze's regime and whose leaders formed the new government later on, was closely attached to the Western democracy-promotion agenda (Angley 2013). Furthermore, Saakashvili himself had perfect relations with neoconservative elites in Washington and openly spoke about the importance of Western standards being applied (Jones 2006; Civil Georgia 2004). And still, the fundamental determinants behind the regime change were corruption and state malfunctioning. Thousands of people rushed to the streets demanding a normal life in a normal country whereas no geopolitical issue has actually been raised (USAID from the American people 2005). For instance, during the Rose revolution Western flags, such as of the US, NATO, and EU, appeared very rarely among the regular protesters.

Moscow, on the other hand, was also actively involved in promoting and supporting the peaceful power transition. Particularly, then-minister of foreign affairs of Russia Igor Ivanov personally attended political protests in Tbilisi and expressed the Kremlin's readiness to help Georgian people to build a stable, peaceful and prosperous state (Al Jazeera 2003). Furthermore, Ivanov flew to Adjara autonomous republic where local leader Aslan Abashidze openly stood up against Saakashvili (EurasiaNet 2004). He significantly contributed to de-escalation, factually directing the newly formed and still highly fragile government to avoid domestic bloodshed. The first serious challenge for the post-Rose revolution elites that may have ended-up by yet another civil confrontation was quietly solved due to political support from the Kremlin (Bransten 2004).

Interestingly, in December 2009 in an interview to the local newspaper Georgian Times, the ousted Eduard Shevardnadze argued that both the US and Russia were willing to replace him (Koridze 2015). According to the former president, he was perceived (or rather hated) by the Kremlin for his role in bringing down the Soviet Union while Washington was looking for a radically pro-Western, hence anti-Russian force in Georgia. Shevardnadze's mission, in turn, as he explained it, was to achieve real sovereignty by keeping the fragile balance between these superpowers via dialogue and diplomacy. So far, according to Shevardnadze, Saakashvili and the Rose Revolution was a joint American-Russian project (ibidem).

The Georgian-Russian political "honeymoon" was strengthened by Saakashvili's openly positive remarks toward the Kremlin, stressing the importance of Georgian-Russian relations and the involvement of the Northern neighbor in setting-up the well-being in Georgia as well as in the whole region.

Finally, the third president of Georgia undertook his first official foreign visit to Moscow in February 2004 where he met Vladimir Putin and discussed inter-state relations. Satisfied by the meeting, both leaders agreed to build a better future by "combined" efforts (Peuch 2004 [1]). Nothing actually indicated anti-Russian narratives or sentiments among Saakashvili and his allies. Likewise, Russian political elites considered the Rose Revolution a good chance to "reset" relations and strengthen cooperation between the governments of Putin and Saakashvili (Clogg 2004). This "reset" policy was unexpectedly cut off due to military confrontation between Georgian armed forces and separatists in Tskhinvali region in July-August 2004 (Peuch 2004 [2]; Civil Georgia 2005). Only through the intervention of international actors, especially the OSCE Mission to Georgia, could the conflict be prevented from escalating (The New York Times 2004).

Arguably, Saakashvili's attempt to solve separatist conflict by "blitzkrieg" tactics, not taking into consideration Moscow's motives and interests, broke the trust between Georgian and Russian leaders. Putin, who inherited an almost dismantled state and was actively building a power vertical and stability in Russia, considered this step as a "betrayal". For him, Saakashvili turned into a person who cannot be trusted. Additionally, it became obvious that Saakashvili and Putin had principally different approaches to nation- and state-building processes: Tbilisi aspired to gain absolute independence, to "run away" from the Kremlin while Moscow, oppositely, attempted to restore regional and global dominance. By the end of the day, Saakashvili's "shock therapy" totally re-shuffled political, economic, academic and civil society elites, leading to an absolute geopolitical shift to a pro-Western foreign policy. Saakashvili's main goal was to create a "new Georgia", free from the Soviet legacy and, from his standpoint, shaped based on the Western-oriented standards (Sikharulidze 2021). This political vision had been heavily influenced by ideological attachment, perception and preferences rather than by the pragmatic and realist approach preached by Eduard Shevardnadze. It has been only further strengthened by Russia's economic embargo, gas wars and other steps undertaken to punish the Georgian government and Georgian people. Instead of retribution, Moscow pushed Tbilisi closer to its American and European allies in an attempt to balance what was considered Russia's aggressive foreign policy. Saakashvili officially asked NATO to get a Membership Action Plan (MAP) and join NATO to protect the state's sovereignty and guarantee security. Instead of a 're-set' Georgian-Russian relations experienced an "overload" which was later cemented by the August 2008 war. The Kremlin recognized Abkhazia and South Ossetia as independent states while Tbilisi cut off diplomatic relations with the Northern neighbor, finalizing its geopolitical turn to the West. Georgia cut the long-lasting chords with Russia and arguably the region as a whole. Georgia's already solid mental detachment from South Caucasus and the post-Soviet space for the sake of Western integration (NATO/EU) termed as "join/re-join the European family" and/or "join the civilized world" is being explained by terms such as "Europeanness" (Kakachia and Minesashvili 2015) and "radical Europeanness" (Sikharulidze 2020). Kakachia and others (2020) hold that despite Georgia's fragile geopolitical position and, in theory, its more pragmatic attachment to the Kremlin, Tbilisi is still devoted to its Western foreign agenda. According to Georgian scholars this is due to the so-called Europeanness combination of European identity of local elites and their preference for liberal democracy and values. Furthermore, Sikharulidze argued that Georgia has gone too far in its aspiration to become a part of the "Western family", thus turning "Europeanness" to "radical Europeanness", meaning total abandonment of its geopolitical interests in the neighborhood as well as demolition of a pro-active pragmatic and grounded foreign policy towards the South Caucasus and the post-Soviet space in general.

Being unable to obtain NATO membership due to two separatist regions, Tbilisi remains solidly committed to its Western agenda, but keeping ties with Russia on the economic level. Diplomatic relations are not on the table until the Kremlin restores Tbilisi's sovereignty. Thus, in the end of the day, Georgia's appraisal against corrupt political system could have ended as yet another regime change ("velvet" revolution) but it gradually turned into "colored revolution", meaning ideological and geopolitical re-orientation of the state toward the West and the Western development model.

Velvet Revolution of Armenia

The failure to achieve effective democratization and modernization in post-Soviet Armenia triggered a protracted democratic transition and led to the inability to overcome the multiple crises of political development, including distribution of power, mobility, identity, political participation and legitimacy (Margaryan and Nikoghosyan 2021). In April 2018 the peaceful process of power transition succeeded through a month-long massive street protest in Yerevan, other major cities, as well as in the centers of concentration of the Armenian Diaspora (Demytrie 2018). After eight years and two consecutive terms in office, then-President Serzh Sargsyan had initiated constitutional reforms (December 2016) to shift the semi-presidential system of government to a parliamentary one. Many believed that the constitutional amendments were proposed for nothing else but to help the President to keep power, as Sargsyan's two terms as President were to expire in April 2018 (ibid.). This allowed an opposition leader, Nikol Pashinyan, to start a comprehensive protest campaign which led to Sargsyan's resignation on 23 April 2018 and formation of a new temporary government with Nikol Pashinyan as the Prime Minister. This peaceful process of power transition received the name "Armenian Velvet Revolution". Snap Parliamentary election held in December 2018 legalized the results of this "Velvet Revolution", as the newly formed political alliance „My Step" with Nikol Pashinyan and his team received the majority in Parliament (REFL 2018).

It is fair to say that the "Velvet Revolution" changed the democratization-modernization nexus in Armenia. As stated above, the former unpopular incumbent Serzh Sargsyan had built his power base on semi-autocracy (Freedom House 2018). After eight years in power, he was trying to keep it by initiating constitutional reforms (Broers

2018). After the "Velvet Revolution" the newly formed Government (from the representative of the former opposition and civil society members) initiated reforms which allowed the Economist to call Armenia the "Country of the year 2018" for its democratic transformations (The Economist 2019). At the same time, Freedom House described the situation in Armenia in the following way: "Armenia is in the midst of a significant transition following mass antigovernment protests and elections in 2018 that forced out an entrenched political elite. The new government has pledged to deal with long-standing problems including systemic corruption, opaque policymaking, a flawed electoral system, and weak rule of law", though still calling the country "partially free" (Freedom House 2019).

At the same time, Armenia's regime change remained a purely domestic issue. No external actor declared explicit support to either Pashinyan and his movement or Sargsyan and his government. Armenia's international partners only called on both sides to keep the demonstrations and responses peaceful. Ingibjörg Sólrún Gísladóttir, then-Director of the OSCE Office for Democratic Institutions and Human Rights (ODIHR), expressed concern about reports of disproportionate use of force by the police against peaceful demonstrators, including minors, as well as widespread detentions in Yerevan and other cities. The official representative of the head of EU diplomacy also called on the Armenian authorities to immediately release all those detained during the protests in Yerevan and start a political dialogue to resolve the internal political crisis in the republic (News-Armenia 2018 [1]). The spokesman of Russia's President, Dmitry Peskov, commented on the demonstrations in Armenia in the following way: "The events in Armenia regarding the actions of the opposition is a domestic issue of that country, and hypothetic discussions about Russia's interference in the situation are irrelevant. That is exclusively Armenia's domestic issue, this is what I can say." (News-Armenia 2018 [2]). On the other hand, the leaders of the "Velvet Revolution" did their best to make it clear both internationally and domestically that the revolution excludes any geopolitical agenda (Mkrtchyan 2019).

The new Government continued the multi-vector foreign policy strategy (inherited from the previous governments) emphasizing that the Velvet Revolution is exclusively about domestic change and does not follow any geopolitical agenda (Ministry of Foreign Affairs of the Republic of Armenia 2020). The idea behind is that Armenia is not going to be exclusively integrated into either Western (for instance, be exclusive part of 'democratic peace' environment) or the "Eastern"/Russia-led security architecture. Instead, it is developing its agenda based on comprehensive and multi-layer cooperation with all centers of hard and soft power—USA, EU, Russia, Iran, and nowadays China, etc. A clear implication of this approach is that Armenia is cooperating with both NATO and CSTO, until recently contributing into NATO mission to Afghanistan (Information Centre on NATO in Armenia 2024), and providing humanitarian support to Russia in Syria (after the Velvet Revolution) (EurasiaNet 2019; Ministry of Foreign Affairs of the Republic of Armenia 2024). This foreign policy doctrine started approximately nineteen years ago by the administration of the second President of Armenia Robert Kocharyan and found itself quite viable till the Second Artsakh war, including the current administration, which took office after the Velvet Revolution. Shortly after the revolution Pashinyan gave an interview to the Russian RT and told the following: "As I keep saying there is no geopolitical or foreign policy related intention in the Armenian Velvet Revolution. And I keep saying there was no geopolitical plot. It was a purely internal process which had to do only with Armenia. This process will not result in a foreign policy U-turn. I say this, because people who made the revolution to happen has no problem with the foreign policy of Armenia, there is no demand to change the foreign policy." (RussiaToday 2018). The issue had specific importance in Armenia's public opinion due to the cases of Georgia and Ukraine. Many in Armenia believed that the Rose and Orange Revolutions (as well as Euromaidan) pushed Tbilisi and Kiev to make a geopolitical U-turn towards the West (aspiring to EU and NATO membership), followed by deterioration of relations with Russia and leading to the Georgian war of 2008 and conflict in Donbas. In the case of Armenia, Russia was (and remains) the main security guarantor, and cooling down the relations with Russia, many believed, would have meant loss of Artsakh and direct military threat from Turkey. Hence, the new Government in Yerevan did its best to make it explicit that the Velvet Revolution did not contain any geopolitical agenda. The continuity of Armenia's foreign and security policy towards the major players after the Velvet Revolution is reflected also in Armenia's new National Security Strategy, signed by Pashinyan in Summer 2020.

However, in late September 2020 Azerbaijan initiated what is called in Armenia the "Second Artsakh war". This war was stopped in the night of 10 November 2020 and resulted in major territorial and strategic losses for the Artsakh side (and as a consequence for Armenia). Indeed, it transformed the geopolitical landscape in the South Caucasus, as it made the major players in the South Caucasus re-evaluate their role and place in the region. Russia in particular, being the main peace broker in this Second Artsakh war, became the key actor and stakeholder not only in the conflict zone, but the whole region. The EU, on the other hand, faced some transformations. For a long period of time its peace and security policy towards Armenia had included mainly domestic political stability, democratic development and economic prosperity. For years, the EU had been supporting the development of good governance, institution building, as well as fostering civil participation and human rights protection in Armenia (EU—Armenia Relations). In July 2021 the EU declared to provide Armenia with 2.6 billion Euros (European Commission 2021). However, the amount was to be spent in the same logic as above programs. At the same time, neither before nor after the Second Artsakh war has the EU ever directly participated in one of the main foreign policy and security issue for Armenia—the Nagorno-Karabakh conflict, relying on the OSCE mechanisms instead (European Council 2020). Indirectly, however, it participated in the peace talks with France as a OSCE Minsk Group Co-Chair along with the USA and Russia. With the 10 November 2020 cease-fire statement signed by the leaders of Armenia, Azerbaijan, and Russia, the future role of the OSCE Minsk Group as the main peace broker remains uncertain (Broers 2021). In particular, the President of Azerbaijan declared the conflict to be resolved (RBK 2020). Though neither his Armenian counterpart nor any international peace broker has confirmed that assumption (The Prime Minister of the Republic of Armenia 2020), it is not clear how the peace talks will continue and what would be the roles of France and the OSCE. As a result, over time the Second Artsakh war might lead to a weaking of the EU positions in the region.

The United States of America, being another major player in the region, demonstrates a steady decline in strategic priorities towards the region (Elamiryan 2019). Türkiye became one of the main beneficiaries of the Second Artsakh war, hugely increasing its presence in Azerbaijan and in the so-called liberated territories. Finally, the results of the Second Artsakh war reveal the gaps in Armenia's security policy implementation. It resulted in Azerbaijan's violation of Armenia's territorial integrity (ArmenPress 2021; REFL 2021), while Armenia has no resources to oppose this violation. The Armenian "Velvet Revolution", which received the name of the "Revolution of Peace and Love", succeeded in providing a peaceful power transition on the domestic level, avoiding geopolitization. However, it did not manage to provide domestic political stability, national dialogue and consolidation, neither did it lead to an effective foreign policy and enhanced cooperation with foreign partners to neutralize external threats and avoid the Second Artsakh War.

Thus, the Velvet Revolution has not changed Armenia's foreign policy strategy, but the Second Artsakh War has transformed the security landscape in the South Caucasus. That, in turn, might lead to the revision of Armenia's foreign policy in the future, meaning re-consideration of the strategic partnership with Russia via deepening cooperation with the Western powers. Hence, Russia's long-lasting strategic ally may start looking for other security guarantors.

Colored versus Velvet: Comparative Analysis

Despite being located in the same comparatively small South Caucasus region, the cases of Georgia and Armenia demonstrate that the outcomes of revolutions can be significantly different. While motives behind both movements were the same, i.e., fight against corruption, abuse of power, lack of accountability and transparency—or simply all aspects of the so-called "failed state", the "revolutionary" processes were totally diverse, including the role of external actors.

Since the beginning, the Rose Revolution in Georgia was highly cherished by grand actors such as the US and Russia. Both sides perceived it as an opportunity to "reset" relations and to align the country to their respective trajectories, either "democratic" (arguably pro-American) or "non-democratic" (arguably pro-Russian). Washington wanted to intervene in the sphere of influence of Russia while Moscow hoped that it could strengthen its grip on Tbilisi via active communication and cooperation with local young leaders. By the end of the day, all sides agreed that Eduard Shevardnadze should leave his post and that peaceful transition was in the interest of everyone. This common agreement on positiveness of the revolution guaranteed a peaceful transition of power as well as a quick and unbloody re-integration of the Adjara region whose leader Aslan Abashidze proclaimed disobedience. Revolutionary movements in Yerevan, on the other hand, were intentionally detached from geopolitical rivalry. The timing as well as the Georgian and the Ukrainian experiences, especially the Euromaidan (Fishwick 2014), motivated the actors to proclaim neutrality. Neither Washington nor Moscow effectively engaged in the domestic affairs of Armenia, waiting for outcomes of the protests. If common agreement to engage determined the successful peaceful transition in Georgia, the same agreement not to engage had the same effect in case of Yerevan. And this is despite regular parallels that are usually drawn between all revolutionary processes in the region and beyond, especially by Russian scholars, experts and politicians (Ponomareva 2016). Obviously, a comparison begs to be made between the leaders of the appraisals Mikhail Saakashvili and Nikol Pashinyan, including their background, affiliation, rhetoric and approaches. This comparison is even more in-demand after statements made by pro-Western Georgian revolutionists and reformers that they were ready to help Mr. Pashinyan to build a "new" Armenia. It was not external intervention that actually determined the "colored" nature of Georgian movement but rather the geopolitical situation on the ground. In the case of Georgia, the US was at the peak of power, unchallenged and fully determined to extend its influence everywhere. On the other hand, Russia was slowly consolidating its political and economic powers after a disastrous economic default, defeat in the First Chechen War and social as well as military collapses of the 90s. Seeing that the US was ready to engage while Russia was unable to counter gave Tbilisi-based political elites the feeling that the country could oppose Moscow's will and turn to the West. This option became even more attractive since the newly elected Saakashvili realized that his hopes to unify Georgia via quick political, social, economic and military reforms were elusive and Moscow would not let Tskhinvali and Abkhazia regions simply be re-integrated without respective reparations,—reparations that were unacceptable for those in power in Tbilisi. On the other hand, the US administration led by George W. Bush pushed for NATO expansion and persuaded both, Saakashvili as well as allies in Europe, that Washington was ready to foot the bill of this foreign policy agenda. This American strength against Russia's weakness was what actually let the Rose Revolution of Georgia become "colored". The country had the political, geopolitical and economic opportunity to make a significant shift from the North to the West. And this re-orientation took place on all levels of everyday life, especially, in the field of education and science.

By comparison, the situation in Armenia was much more complex. The end of history as proclaimed by the US-based scholar Francis Fukuyama had ended (Fukuyama 2003). Liberal democracies had not conquered the globe while the US-led West significantly weakened its positions. Arguably, unsuccessful military missions in Afghanistan and Iraq, revolutions in Kyrgyzstan and Ukraine (2003) in combination with the mainly failed Arab Spring only contributed to the inability of the West to maintain the post-Soviet world order. At the same time, Russian president Vladimir Putin brought back the country on the global political stage and started fiercely defending national interests. The invasion to Georgia in 2008, annexation of Crimea (2014) and support of separatist movements in Luhansk and Donbas regions of Ukraine only proved that Moscow was motivated to counter the West and re-shape global politics. Taking into consideration this strained geopolitical situation, Yerevan had actually no true alternative to strategic relations, i.e., cooperation with Russia. Any involvement of the Western powers could have led to disastrous events in Nagorno-Karabakh, the symbol of Armenia's dominance over Azerbaijan and great historic victory. Additionally, Türkiye as the second largest NATO member country has strengthened its position in the region, becoming a key ally of Azerbaijan in Baku's aspirations to restore control over the long-lost territories. Türkiye became an independent player in the region, making it overcomplicated for the West to deal with, especially in light of Türkiye's NATO membership, its general strategic importance and the ongoing 'on the edge' confrontation with Russia. Finally, Georgia's shift to the West itself was not perceived as a real success story due to the inability of the country to join NATO and/or EU despite active reforms and assurances over the last two decades. Moreover, the strategic allies of Tbilisi had not managed to protect it against the Russian aggression during the so-called Five Days War. So far, local political elites who were aware of the power disposition were simply incapable of pushing the idea of the geopolitical shift from Russia to the West. The West was simply not perceived and considered as an actual, real alternative to Russian security guarantees. As a result, of course, some pro-Western sentiments were introduced but no real political, social, economic and military shifts were made. Yerevan became the "hostage" of its own necessity to assure the presence of Russia for the sake of Nagorno-Karabakh, on the one hand, and the global geopolitical situation in general, on the other hand. Absence of key determinants for "colored" revolution during and in the aftermath of the protests led to something that was merely regime change without those significant internal changes, reforms that had taken place in Georgia. Neither the US nor the EU was capable of giving Yerevan the same assurances that they used to for Georgia; no more uncrossable "red lines" for Russia in the South Caucasus (The Guardian 2005). Thus, the Armenian revolution was and still is widely regarded as a "velvet".

Conclusion

The cases of the Georgian Revolution of Roses and the Armenian Velvet Revolution reveal the current strategic environment in the South Caucasus through the lenses of radical domestic political transformations which took place eighteen and five years ago respectively. In the case of Georgia almost two decades have gone by, but the geopolitical results of the post-Revolution of Roses events still determine foreign policy priorities of the country and its relations with Russia. In the case of the Armenian Velvet Revolution, it faced the Second Artsakh war, though it is still not clear whether the war was provoked by the revolution. Only the recent offensive of Azerbaijan that led to the collapse of the de-facto Republic of Artsakh may significantly affect relations between Yerevan and Moscow. But possible consequences are hardly predictable for now and even if geopolitical changes will take place they can hardly be perceived as direct outcomes of the Armenian revolution of 2018.

The above allows us to draw the following conclusions:

Firstly, the conceptual difference between "colored" and "velvet" revolutions (in case of political processes in Georgia and Armenia) is about geopolitical agenda and/or outcomes. "Colored" revolutions are mainly about open or hidden geopolitical agenda, frequently accompanied by the presence of external actors and, as a consequence, leading to U-turns in foreign policy. In case of "velvet" revolutions, there is the absence of such geopolitical motives with no explicit involvement of external actors. As a consequence, "velvet" revolutions do not support geopolitical U-turns. As we saw in the case of Georgia, a variety of external actors did their best to impact the revolution. In the case of Armenia, the international community kept silent and characterized the revolution as Armenia's domestic issue.

Secondly, in both cases the revolutions started as social and economic movements against corruption, poor economic conditions, as well as social injustice. However, in less than five years the Georgian Revolution received a geopolitical "face". In the case of Armenia, in five years since 2018 there has been no radical transformation in geopolitical activities of political elites in Yerevan. Moreover, during the snap Parliamentary elections (20 June 2021) all major political forces were stating their commitment to improve relations with Russia. On the other hand, it is a bit early to judge, as the results of the recent war can change the perceptions of political leaders in Yerevan.

Finally, in both cases the relations with Russia were perceived, inter alia, through the lenses of ethnopolitical conflicts. However, Saakashvili made a geopolitical U-turn as soon as he realized that Russia is not going to follow his plan to integrate Abkhazia and South Ossetia. On the contrary, after the Second Artsakh war, Armenia had been prolonging its security cooperation with Russia, though it was expecting more help from Russia during the war. The situation changed just recently, sparking anti-Russian sentiments on the ground. Some Western experts and scholars even argue that this is the end for the Yerevan-Moscow strategic partnership. But whether Armenia can actually diversify its security, detach from Moscow and align itself with the Western world is still to be seen.

Thus, despite being located in the same region and facing the consequences of ethno-political conflicts, Georgia and Armenia took rather diverse paths in their foreign and security policy making. This can be explained, particularly, by two reasons. On the one hand, there are various security-threat nexus perception by the two states. Particularly, in the case of Georgia, the country started to extend cooperation to Türkiye and Azerbaijan to counter-balance Russia. In the case of Armenia, it is very complicated to develop that scenario due to the variety of political and geopolitical problems Armenia has with both countries.

At the same time, there is a transformation of the geopolitical landscape in the South Caucasus over the last 20 years. During 2000-2010, the West has been much more active in the region, providing the opportunity for "geopolitical alternative" for Georgia. For now, Armenia will face hard times if it starts searching for geopolitical alternatives to Russia.

Bibliography

Al Jazeera. 2003. *Russia Mediates in Georgia Storm*. https://www.aljazeera.com/news/2003/11/23/russia-mediates-in-georgia-storm.

Angley, Robyn E. 2013. *Escaping the Kmara Box: Reframing the Role of Civil Society in Georgia's Rose Revolution*, Studies of Transition States and Societies, Vol. 5, Is. 1, https://core.ac.uk/download/pdf/270289546.pdf.

ArmenPress. 2021. *Azerbaijani Military's Illegal Presence in Territory of Black Lake Grossly Violates Rights of Armenian Border Residents*. https://armenpress.am/eng/news/1052160.html.

BBC News. 2005. *How the Rose Revolution Happened*. 2005. http://news.bbc.co.uk/2/hi/4532539.stm.

Bransten, Jeremy. 2004. *Georgia: Adjara Standoff Ends with Abashidze Relinquishing Power*, REFL, https://www.rferl.org/a/1052660.html.

Civil Georgia. 2004. *Remarks by George W. Bush and Mikheil Saakashvili*. https://civil.ge/archives/105333.

Civil Georgia. 2005. *Igor Ivanov: Georgia's Rose Revolution "against Values and Principles" of CoE, OSCE*. https://civil.ge/archives/185355.

Clogg, Rachel. 2004. *The Rose Revolution and the Georgian-Abkhazian Conflict: Light at the End of the Tunnel?* Conciliation Resources, Is. 24, https://rc-services-assets.s3.eu-west-1.amazonaws.com/s3fs-public/RoseRevolutionandGeorgian-Abkhazian%20Conflict_200405_ENG.pdf.

Coffey, Luke. 2020. *Georgia's Balancing Act in the South Caucasus.* The Middle East Institute, https://www.mei.edu/publications/georgias-balancing-act-south-caucasus.

Companjen, Francoise J., Gogheliani, Tina, Khutsishvili, George, Mkhelidze, Zurab, Mshvidobadze, Rusudan, Nizharadze, George, Nowak, Heiko and Piralishvili, Zaza. 2008. *Civil Society and the Rose Revolution in Georgia.* International Centre on Conflict and Negotiation, http://www.iccn.ge/files/iccn_rose_revolution_book_eng_full_2008.pdf.

Elamiryan, Ruben. 2019. *Eastern Partnership Countries on the Cross-Roads of the Eurasian Geopolitics: USA, European Union (EU), Russia, and China.* Think Visegrad. https://think.visegradfund.org/wp-content/uploads/think_visegrad_analysis_ruben_elamiryan_ifat_2017.pdf.

EurasiaNet. 2004. *Ajaria Declares State of Emergency, Georgian Leadership Urges Regional Inhabitants to Disobey Curfew.* https://www.refworld.org/docid/46a484e5b.html.

EurasiaNet. 2019. *Armenia Sends Military Deminers and Medics to Support Russian Mission in Syria.* https://eurasianet.org/armenia-sends-military-deminers-and-medics-to-support-russian-mission-in-syria.

European Commission. 2021. *Armenia: Remarks by Commissioner Olivér Várhelyi at the Press Point with Acting Deputy Prime Minister Mher Grigoryan.* https://ec.europa.eu/commission/commissioners/2019-2024/varhelyi/announcements/armenia-remarks-commissioner-oliver-varhelyi-press-point-acting-deputy-prime-minister-mher-grigoryan_en.

European Council. 2020. *Nagorno-Karabakh: Declaration by the High Representative on behalf of the European Union.* https://www.consilium.europa.eu/en/press/press-releases/2020/11/19/nagorno-karabakh-declaration-by-the-high-representative-on-behalf-of-the-european-union/.

Fishwick, Carmen, 2014. *'We Were so Naive and Optimistic': Ukraine Euromaidan Protesters Tell Us What's Changed For Them.* The Guardian: https://www.theguardian.com/world/2014/mar/04/ukraine-crisis-protesters-kiev-euromaidan-independence-square.

Freedom House. *Freedom in the World 2016-9: Armenia.* https://freedomouse.org/report/freedom-world/2019/Armenia.

Fukuyama, Francis, 1989. *The End of History?* The National Interest. No. 16 (Summer 1989), pp. 3-18, https://www.jstor.org/stable/24027184.

Information Centre on NATO in Armenia. 2024 [accessed]. *NATO-Armenia Relations*. http://www.natoinfo.am/en/armenia-nato-relations/.

Jones, Stephen. 2006. *The Rose Revolution: A Revolution without Revolutionaries?* Cambridge Review of International Affairs: Vol. 19, Is. 1, https://doi.org/10.1080/09557570500501754.

Kakachia, Kornely and Salome Minesashvili. 2015. *"Identity Politics: Exploring Georgian Foreign Policy Behavior."* Journal of Eurasian Studies: 6, no. 2, pp. 171-180, https://doi.org/10.1016/j.euras.2015.04.002.

Kandelaki, Giorgi. 2006. *Georgia's Rose Revolution. A Participant's Perspective.* Special Report. United States Institute of Peace, https://www.usip.org/sites/default/files/sr167.pdf.

Kakachia, Kornely, Lebanidze, Bidzina and Dzebisashvili, Shalva. 2020. *Game of (Open) Doors: NATO-Georgian Relations and Challenges for Sustainable Partnership*. Georgian Institute of Politics, https://gip.ge/publication-post/game-of-open-doors-nato-georgian-relations-and-challenges-for-sustainable-partnership/.

Laurence, Broers, 2018. *In Armenia, a Constitutional Power Grab Backfires.* Chatham House, https://www.chathamhouse.org/2018/04/armenia-constitutional-power-grab-backfires.

Laurence, Broers. 2021. *The OSCE's Minsk Group: A Unipolar Artifact in a Multipolar World.* EurasiaNet, https://eurasianet.org/perspectives-the-osces-minsk-group-a-unipolar-artifact-in-a-multipolar-world.

Lomsadze, Giorgi. 2021. *Not All Roads Lead to Georgia.* EurasiaNet, https://eurasianet.org/not-all-roads-lead-to-georgia.

MacFarlane, Neil. 2011. *Post-Revolutionary Georgia on the Edge?* Chatham House, https://www.chathamhouse.org/sites/default/files/public/Research/Russia%20and%20Eurasia/bp0311_macfarlane.pdf.

Margaryan, Mariam and Nikoghosyan, Lusyne. 2021. *The Problems of Identity Transformation in the Process of Political Modernization.* Public Administration Academy of the Republic of Armenia, pp. 184-193, https://mmmargaryan.wordpress.com/2021/07/26/the-problems-of-identity-transformation-in-the-process-of-political-modernization/.

Markozashvili, Lasha. 2014. *Transition Toward Democracy—Georgian Problems.* Przegląd Politologiczny, pp. 185-202, https://pressto.amu.edu.pl/index.php/pp/article/view/2939.

Ministry of Foreign Affairs of the Republic of Armenia. 2024 [accessed]. *International Organisations: Collective Security Treaty Organization.* https://www.mfa.am/en/international-organisations/1.

Ministry of Foreign Affairs of the Republic of Armenia. 2020 [accessed]. *National Security Strategy of the Republic of Armenia.* https://www.mfa.am/filemanager/security%20and%20defense/Armenia%202020%20National%20Security%20Strategy.pdf.

Mitchell, Lincoln. 2009. *Uncertain Democracy.* University of Pennsylvania Press, pp. 43-78.

Mkrtchyan, Marianna. 2019. *Mnatsakanyan: Velvet Revolution in Armenia does not have any Geopolitical Overtones.* ArmInfo—Information Company, https://arminfo.info/full_news.php?id=41387&lang=3.

Peuch, Jean-Christophe (1). 2004. *Deadliest Fighting in Years Erupts in South Ossetia.* REFL, https://www.rferl.org/a/1054281.html.

Peuch, Jean-Christophe. (2) 2004. *Georgia: Saakashvili in Moscow, Looking to Start Ties with A Clean Slate.* REFL, https://www.rferl.org/a/1051504.html.

Rayhan, Demytrie. 2018. *Why Armenia 'Velvet Revolution' Won Without a Bullet Fired.* BBC News, https://www.bbc.com/news/world-europe-43948181.

RBK. 2020. *Aliyev Declared About Final Solution in Nagorno-Karabakh.* https://www.rbc.ru/rbcfreenews/5fa9d1229a79471d4352119c.

REFL. 2018. *Pashinian Alliance Scores 'Revolutionary Majority' In Landslide Armenian Win.* https://www.rferl.org/a/armenian-elections-pashinian-my-step-sarkisian-hhk/29645721.html.

REFL. 2021. *Yerevan Accuses Azerbaijan of Blocking Major Road Connecting Two Parts of Armenian Region.* https://www.rferl.org/a/armenia-azerbaijan-blocks-road/31429111.html.

RussiaToday. 2018. *EU Relations Won't Come at Expense of Russian Ties—Armenian PM.* https://www.rt.com/shows/rt-interview/429873-pashinyan-armenia-interview-russia/.

Sikharulidze, Archil. 2020. *Georgia Beyond "Radical Europeanness": Undiscovered Directions of Foreign Policy.* Journal of International Analytics: Vol. 11, No. 2, https://www.interanalytics.org/jour/article/view/283.

The Economist. *The Economist's Country of the Year 2018.* https://www.economist.com/leaders/2018/12/22/the-economists-country-of-the-year-2018.

The Guardian. 2005. *Bush Hails Georgia as 'Beacon of Liberty'.* https://www.theguardian.com/world/2005/may/10/georgia.usa.

The Jamestown Foundation. 1997. *Georgia's Membership in CIS will Depend on Russian Policies.* https://jamestown.org/program/georgias-membership-in-cis-will-depend-on-russian-policies/.

The Jamestown Foundation. 2000. *Georgia Knock-Knock-Knocking at NATO's Door.* Vol. 6, Is. 5, https://jamestown.org/program/georgia-knock-knock-knocking-at-natos-door/.

The New York Times. 2004. *Georgia and Separatist Region Close to an Official Cease-Fire.* https://www.nytimes.com/2004/08/14/world/georgia-and-separatist-region-close-to-an-official-cease-fire.html.

The Prime Minister of the Republic of Armenia. 2020. *Prime Minister: "The Joint Statement Provides for the Return to their Homes for People Living in the Regions of Nagorno-Karabakh".* https://www.primeminister.am/en/interviews-and-press-conferences/item/2020/11/25/Nikol-Pashinyan-interview-TACC/.

The World Bank Group. 2012. *Fighting Corruption in Public Services: Chronicling Georgia's Reforms.* Directions in Development: Public Sector Governance Washington, D.C., http://documents.worldbank.org/curated/en/518301468256183463/Fighting-corruption-in-public-services-chronicling-Georgias-reforms.

Troianovski, Anton. 2020. *In Bitter Nagorno-Karabakh War, a Reordering of Regional Powers.* The New York Times, https://www.nytimes.com/2020/11/10/world/europe/armenia-azerbaijan-nagorno-karabakh.html.

USAID from the American People. 2005. *Georgia: Causes of the Rose Revolution and Lessons for Democracy Assistance.* https://csis-website-prod.s3.amazonaws.com/s3fs-public/legacy_files/files/media/csis/pubs/ci.causesroserevolution.03.05.pdf.

ქორიძე, თემური. 2015. სააკაშვილი რუსეთ-ამერიკის ერთობლივი პროექტი იყო, მის შემცვლელს ეძებენ, დარწმუნებული ვარ, ისიც რუსულ-ამერიკული პროექტი იქნება—ედუარდ შევარდნაძე [Koridze, Temuri. 2015. Saakashvili was Russian-American joint project; they are looking for his substitute now and I am sure he will also be Russian-American joint project—Eduard Shevardnadze]. Georgian Times, https://geotimes.com.ge/?m=5&news_id=96159.

Новости-Армения (1). 2018. Хроника "бархатной" революции в Армении: как она свершилась [News-Armenia (1). 2018. Chronicles of Velvet Revolution in Armenia: How it happened], https://newsarmenia.am/news/analytics/khronika-barkhatnoy-revolyutsii-v-armenii-kak-ona-svershilas/.

Новости-Армения (2). 2018. Песков: события в Армении являются внутренним делом этой страны [News-Armenia (2). Peskov: Events in Armenia are domestic business of that country], https://newsarmenia.am/news/armenia/peskov-sobytiya-v-armenii-yavlyayutsya-vnutrennim-delom-etoy-strany/.

Понаморева, Елена., 2016. *Что такое Цветные революции и как с ними бороться?* Представительная власть? №1-2. С. 26-38 [Ponomareva, Elena, 2016. *What are the Colored Revolutions and How to Fight them?* Representative Power (Government): №1-2, pp. 26-38], https://mgimo.ru/library/publications/chto_takoe_tsvetnye_revolyutsii_i_kak_s_nimi_borotsya/.

Challenges of European Integration: The Cases of Armenia and Georgia

Anahit Babayan

Abstract

The South Caucasus is a region characterized by a number of challenges: democratization and institution-building initiatives, human rights and rule of law, legal and judicial problems, economic problems, civil society. However the main challenges are ethnic conflicts and security. Analyzing the above-mentioned challenges, this chapter describes how the EU responds to these challenges in Armenia and Georgia. The goal of this chapter is to highlight the role of Europeanization in the context of overcoming these challenges. Its main finding is that the EU is trying to play an active role by maintaining close relations with all parties concerned. But better public participation, awareness-raising, comprehensive knowledge and understanding of the EU in Armenia and Georgia, particularly among civil society organizations, are needed for reaching a success.

Keywords: Armenia; Georgia; European Union; South Caucasus; Challenges of Europeanization.

Introduction

Since the collapse of the Soviet Union, the three newly independent states of the South Caucasus need to overcome many challenges. Europeanization was widely seen as the "platform" through which the states would address those challenges, taking into account the fact that the South Caucasus has been in the focus of the EU's attention for some time. The EU's value-based approach emphasizes democracy, rule of law and respect for human rights. The European Neighborhood Policy (ENP) and the Eastern Partnership (EaP) are its main mechanisms and participating states are receiving a wide array of support. In the case of Georgia, the main legal foundation is the Association Agreement (AA) with the EU. Armenia, by comparison, has founded its relations with the EU on a Comprehensive and Enhanced Partnership Agreement (CEPA). Whereas the AA with Georgia has a membership perspective, CEPA does not, as Armenia is a member state of the Eurasian Economic Union (EAEU). The purpose of the chapter is to reflect and analyze the challenges of democratization, rule of law and security for Armenia and Georgia and their possible solutions.

Armenia: Challenges of European Integration

Democracy and Human Rights

After independence, the Republic of Armenia actively developed bilateral relations with the EU. In the beginning, relations were founded on a Partnership and Cooperation Agreement (PCA) which was signed in 1996 and entered into force in 1999. The PCA provided opportunities for Armenia to promote political and economic cooperation and also to develop a dialogue with the EU. In addition, Armenia engaged in various EU assistance programs: TACIS (Technical Assistance to the Commonwealth of Independent States), TRACECA (Transport Corridor: Europe, Caucasus, Asia), INOGATE. Later, Armenia was involved in a number of other EU assistance programs, such as ERASMUS+, TEMPUS, TAIEX, TWINNING, HORIZON 2020, COSME (Competitiveness of Enterprises and Small and Medium-sized Enterprises), EU4Digital (four projects are funded under the EU4Digital Initiative— the EU4Digital Facility, EaPConnect, EU4Digital Cyber and EU4Digital Broadband. Besides, the EU supports a number of other projects that contribute to the digital economy and society at both regional and bilateral (country) levels.

In Armenia, Jean Monnet activities are being implemented to promote excellence in teaching and research in the field of European Studies. These actions also aim at fostering dialogue between the academic world and policymakers, particularly with the aim of enhancing the governance of EU policies. European Studies comprise the study of Europe in its entirety with particular emphasis on the European integration process in both its internal and external aspects. Through such programs communities, especially young people, are invited to acknowledge the history, values and goals of the EU. This is really important, because unlike Georgia, Armenian people know very little about the EU, and the path of European integration in Armenia is weakly developed.

The EU is a key reform partner of Armenia. Following the Armenian 'Velvet Revolution' of 2018, the EU stepped up its support and increased its annual allocation in grants to €65 million in 2019.[i] The new authorities engaged in reform processes in the areas of human rights, the rule of law, and the establishment of democracy. These reforms were noticeable in recording results in the fight against corruption, freedom of speech, a new understanding of the role of civil society, activism, and so on (Rakopyan 2019, 544). On 20 June 2021, after the 44-day war, the Armenian people again had an election of the National Assembly. Support for elections is a key component in the development of democracy. Through EU support civil society organizations were able to provide accessibility of information to voters, especially to women and people with disabilities, also observation missions were carried out in Yerevan and regions[ii] which contributed to free and fair elections.

The Nagorno-Karabakh Conflict and the Security Challenge for Armenia

The Nagorno-Karabakh conflict as an ethnic conflict reached its pinnacle in 2020 when Azerbaijan started a full-scale war, with Türkiye as its supporter. Throughout the war which lasted 44 days, Türkiye helped Azerbaijan by all possible means. Besides, mercenary terrorists were transferred from Syria to fight in the line of the Azerbaijani army (De Waal 2021, 5) and this entire arsenal was used against Armenians, openly showing their desire to annihilate Armenians. The war ended with the Agreement signed on 9 November 2022. According to the Agreement there were territorial concessions to Azerbaijan and Russian peacekeepers were deployed in Nagorno-Karabakh. Up to now, hostilities have not stopped: neither in Nagorno-Karabakh nor at the Armenian-Azerbaijani border. On 13 September 2022, Azerbaijan launched a large-scale attack against the sovereign territory of Armenia. The units of the Azerbaijani armed forces engaged in intense artillery fire against Armenian positions and the settlements of Goris, Kapan, Sotk, Jermuk, Artanish and Ishkhanasar. Azerbaijanis targeted the civilians with the goal of depopulating the border villages.

Needless to say, such an anti-Armenian, belligerent policy leads to human casualties, undermines regional security and peace, and leads to humanitarian issues threating Armenia's security. On 15 December 2022, under the guise of so-called "environmental activists", Azerbaijan closed the Lachin Corridor, the only road connecting Artsakh to the world, and caused a humanitarian disaster. Also gas and electricity supplies are regularly stopped, people's rights are violated. Armenia has instituted proceedings against Azerbaijan. The Court has issued a legally binding order[iii] against Azerbaijan in the proceedings brought by Armenia against it, while categorically rejecting Azerbaijan's requests made in the parallel proceedings Azerbaijan brought against Armenia. In the mentioned order, the Court found that there is an imminent risk of irreparable harm to Armenians' rights under the Convention on the Elimination of All Forms Racial Discrimination (CERD), and ordered Azerbaijan to take all necessary measures to ensure unimpeded movement of persons, vehicles and cargo along the Lachin Corridor in both directions. Baku also makes territorial claims against Syunik and that without the consent of the Armenians they will open the Zangezur Corridor which will be ready in 2024.[iv] It involves not only the construction of a highway, but also a railway, and according to Azerbaijan's demand, it should not come under the control of Armenia. If Azerbaijan succeeds in carrying out its goals in Nagorno-Karabakh and Armenia after that Armenian people will face a serious security threat.

Armenia-EU Relations

The EU's interest in the South Caucasus is most clearly expressed in the ENP and EaP policy formats (Lynch 2003, 173-174). By joining the ENP, Armenia acquired the opportunity to establish intensive political, economic, security, and cultural relations with the EU by including issues such as developing democratic structures, the rule of law, judicial reforms and combating corruption, respect for human rights and fundamental freedoms, economic development as well as poverty reduction, environmental protection, improvement of the investment climate, convergence of economic legislation and administrative practices, and the development of energy strategy (Mkrtchyan et al. 2009, 15).

The EaP, based on the existing ENP framework, tries to create the necessary conditions for further deepening of political association and economic integration between the EU and partner countries—Armenia, Georgia, Azerbaijan, the Republic of Moldova, the Republic of Belarus, and Ukraine (Eastern Partnership Summit 2009, 6). The original plan was to conclude AAs and Deep and Comprehensive Free Trade Agreements (DCFTAs) between the EaP partner countries and the EU. They were to replace the PCAs, with the main aim of creating the necessary conditions for accelerating political association and deepening economic integration based on the "more for more" formula. Armenia was well under way to sign the AA, but on 3 September 2013 Armenia withdrew from the AA negotiation process and joined the Customs Union and later the EAEU because of the leverage of Russian influence. Despite joining the integration structures in the post-Soviet area, however, Armenia was ready to sign a new agreement. This policy was realized in November 2017 with the signing of CEPA. Being confronted by difficult geopolitical choices, Armenia thus emerged as a laboratory to observe and study the intertwined processes of post-Soviet transformation, internationalization, Europeanization and regional integration of different levels and vectors (Khovorostyankina 2017, 47).

On 10 February 2021, Armenia was notified about the completion of the ratification process of CEPA by the EU and EU Member States. The Agreement entered into force on March 1 of this year. Accordingly, bilateral relations are regulated by CEPA, replacing the PCA and becoming a unique legal instrument that regulates relations between the EU and other member of the EAEU. CEPA is a considerable achievement for Armenia in deepening relations with the EU. It aims at strengthening political, economic partnership and cooperation, maintaining and strengthening peace at regional and international levels, expanding cooperation in the fields of freedom, security, justice, contributing to democracy and political, economic, and institutional stability, guaranteeing further progress in judicial and legal reforms in such a way as to ensure the independence, quality, and efficiency of the system, and creating favorable conditions in areas of mutual interests. The Agreement is also an opportunity to achieve modernization based on conducting free and fair elections, a fair trial, and respect for human rights. For the successful implementation of CEPA, four key points are identified: better living standards (new jobs, more business opportunities), a fairer and safer society (strengthened democracy and human rights, more safety and security for citizens, more transparency), cleaner environment (more protected environment, cleaner, and affordable energy), more choice in education (better education, more opportunities for research).[v] CEPA thus became a tool offered by the EU to a country with no membership perspective. Armenia has undertaken reciprocal obligations under the Agreement, only the fulfillment of which can allow Armenia to make progress in these areas. Armenia-EU dialogue is developing in areas where this dialogue is combined with Armenia's commitments under the EAEU. Commitments within the EAEU, on the other hand, leave very little space for Armenia in deepening cooperation with the EU, in particular, in the economic sphere. By joining the EAEU, Armenia was largely deprived of the opportunity to pursue an independent foreign trade and economic policy, delegating that competency to the EAEU (Dragneva and Wolczuk 2017, 17). In other words, Armenia's "hands" are tied when it comes to concluding trade deals with the other party. It is noteworthy that in order to ensure the stability of the values underlying CEPA during the negotiations, the EU rejected the "carve-out clause" proposed by the Armenian side which would allow Armenia to refuse to fulfill its obligations under CEPA in areas where the EAEU could have adopted new provisions (Kostanyan and Giragosyan 2017, 7). This means that the negotiators of CEPA relied on the text of the failed EU-Armenia AA to bring it into line with the new format of EU-Armenia relations. The rejection of the "carve-out clause" by the EU can also be considered a "warning" to Armenia that implementing CEPA should not be compromised by Armenian-Russian relations, in particular by the Armenia-EAEU integration process. Due to all of this, Armenia is trying to maintain a coordinated policy, on the one hand, by joining the international integration structures formed in the post-Soviet space (EAEU as well as the Collective Security Treaty Organization, CSTO), and on the other hand, establishing effective cooperation relations under CEPA. Such a complementary policy would enable Armenia to expand its ability to maneuver and preclude it from moving deeper into the orbit of Russian influence (Terzyan 2016, 153). The current and former authorities of Armenia adopted the complementary policy for keeping relations with the EU as well as continuing to be a member of the EAEU. Unlike the changes that took place in the realm of domestic policy, the foreign policy discourse did not undergo significant changes. Only the leader of the revolution, Nikol Pashinyan, who was known as an opposition deputy and called for leaving the EAEU, stated as a justification that after joining the EAEU, the Republic of Armenia experienced economic, social and military-political regression. Yet, from the very beginning of his tenure Pashinyan fundamentally changed his stance on the EAEU and on the Armenian-Russian partnership. During the first meeting with the Russian President, Pashinyan noted in particularly: "We have things to discuss, but there are also things that do not need any discussion. That is the strategic relationship of allies between Armenia and Russia ... I can assure you that in Armenia there is a consensus, and nobody has ever doubted the importance of the strategic nature of Armenian-Russian relations" (Reuters, 2018). This shows that the foreign policy priorities of the new government remained largely in line with the foreign policy of the previous governments.

It must be noted that Armenia's foreign policy is greatly influenced by the constant threats to security and the levers of influence by Russia. First, Russia is Armenia's main economic partner; second, Armenia is highly dependent on energy supplies from Russia; third, Armenian communities in Russia (Terzyan 2015, 256). The search for security guarantees forces Armenia to make its foreign policy situational, that is, Armenia takes any decision depending on the situation. If Armenia's hands are tied in a separate economic sphere, then security has a complete impact on Armenia's foreign and domestic policy. Security is the challenge that makes Armenia dependent on Russia. Although Armenia is trying to diversify its environment of security guarantees, Russia remains the main guarantor (Ghazaryan and Delcour 2018, 5-6). Armenia has always been in Russia's sphere of interest: without Armenia, it would be almost impossible for Russia to maintain its presence and influence in the South Caucasus. The EU views CEPA as an agreement with a country with no membership prospects, unlike Georgia, Ukraine and Moldova, which have signed AAs. CEPA as opposed to an AA does not imply a gradual rapprochement, but instead develops and strengthens political dialogue in areas of mutual interest, viewing the EU as a key partner in modernization (Delcour and Wolczuk 2015, 500). Work is currently underway on the legal approximation to CEPA, which is a lengthy phased process in accordance with the agreement's roadmap.[vi] The EU was involved in the 2020-2022 National Strategy for the Protection of Human Rights and actively supported the review of the judicial-legal strategy.[vii] This means that the previous cooperation has been assessed successfully and Armenia is fulfilling its obligations under CEPA. Within the framework of CEPA, the creative acceleration program "CATAPULT" was launched which aims to promote the cultural and creative production sectors. The EU also tries to work with Armenia in terms of strengthening the intellectual property rights protection system. This will enable Armenian companies, artists and cultural representatives to rely on strong intellectual property rights protection systems in Armenia. This is important for selling high-quality cultural, creative and innovative products and attracting foreign direct investments to Armenia.

Georgia: Challenges of European Integration

Democratic Process and Development

After several decades of independence, Georgian people are going through a very complicated process to come closer to the developed world. Despite numerous obstacles from foreign powers and internal misunderstandings, Georgians are still very much inclined to become part of the European society and have the aspiration to be accepted to the North Atlantic space.[viii] Those attitudes are well-developed, especially among young people who get an education on the European way of life, have access to information on social media and most importantly, have the opportunity to travel, study and live in the EU and understand what a real European society in practice means. There is a big tendency among Georgian people to move to Europe actively. In the National Security Concept of Georgia it is mentioned that the USA is their strategic partner and they will strive for membership in EU and NATO.

However, the democratic process in Georgia really means a permanent political crisis, a weak party system and a lack of power transitions in the country's political life. In three decades of Georgian history, power transitions have happened three times and two times on the verge of violent protest. Even the elections of 2021, especially their 2nd round, raised many questions for international observers who published very harsh statements about its standards.[ix] The OSCE spoke of "sharp imbalances in resources, and an undue advantage of incumbency further benefited the ruling party and tilted the playing field" (OSCE, Election observation mission 2021, n. p.) when characterizing the second-round election of October 30. This criticism by international observers spurred the Georgian opposition not to accept the results and follow the path of street protest which, however, destabilizes the political environment and hampers the development of the system even further. So, an unbiased observer will hardly expect to find the possibility of a peaceful power transition in Georgia in the near future.

Economic Situation

2016 was a year of hope when the DCFTA between the EU and Georgia entered into force.[x] Experts, analysts and common people very strongly anticipated that this agreement would tie Georgia more closely to the EU and improve the economic environment inside the country. In 2016, before the DCFTA was implemented, the share of Georgia's exports to the EU was 26 %. The agreement should have pushed and stimulated Georgian producers and government as well helped them to find some niches in EU markets. But the reality turned out to be quite different. Specifically, after more than five years of DCFTA implementation the level of exports to the EU has dropped to 15,9 %. One of the main reasons is the switching from European markets to other ones, although those other markets are very risky and not as trustworthy as they might seem. For example, according to the National Statistics Office of Georgia, in the period January-October 2021 Georgia's largest share of trade was with the EAEU at 47.6 %. China holds the first position at 15.3 % as a major export partner and Russia is the second at 14.2 % (National Statistics Office of Georgia 2021, n. p.). Obviously, this level of trade relations creates a risky environment in terms of dependency on perilous, autocratic regimes. For example, Georgia is very much dependent on products imported from the EAEU, Russia (10,8 %) and China (8.9 %) (National Statistics Office of Georgia 2021, n. p). This means that a significant share of the commodities used by Georgian citizens are produced in or exported from the countries with inimical or in some ways ambiguous attitudes toward Georgia and its geopolitical trajectory.

Judicial System

The judicial system is beyond criticism in Georgian reality for more than three decades. Strengthening it and making it more democratic, transparent and unbiased has been a top demand of the EU, and the EU has supported relevant policies in many ways. Another example is the Council of Europe's project "Georgia—Support to the Implementation of the Judicial Reform" in 2016-2019 (Council of Europe 2021, n. p). Also, the Venice Commission gave numerous indications and recommendations toward the Georgian Government and the High Council of Justice of Georgia. The EU actively called on the Georgian Government to make the appointment process of the Supreme Court Justices transparent and to guarantee equal treatment to all candidates. But, by a collective letter, Georgian judges considered this recommendation a violation of the independence and sovereignty of the Georgian court system (Zedelashvili 2021, n. p). After that, the EU withheld a macro-financial loan worth EUR 75 million to the Georgian Government in the context of Covid-19 pandemic.[xi] The lack of judicial independence hinders political reforms and democratic processes. Moreover, it discredits the country on the international level. Georgian society experienced those controversies very painfully during the previous years when the international community singlehandedly recognized that the Georgian Government had several political prisoners who were pardoned by the President only after long-time political pressure.[xii] Until now, the largest opposition party claims that former president Saakashvili is a political prisoner, and it is supported in this claim by members of the European Parliament who warn that his imprisonment could be of a "political nature".[xiii] That is why opposition parties and civil society actively accuse the Georgian court system of being biased and partial. This process damages Georgia as a country and leads to the deterioration of everyday life of the common people whose economic and social conditions are falling behind.

Georgia-EU Relations

Georgia has been striving to join the EU from the very first day of its independence. Georgia's Government at the time officially declared this goal in the early 1990s, and virtually every government and ruling party that has followed has reaffirmed that the country's main priority was its integration into the EU. In 2004, Georgia, as a result of the "Rose Revolution", received an invitation to participate in the ENP. Furthermore, despite the fact that the main priority of the new government in terms of foreign policy was to acquire NATO membership, institutional integration into the EU was also a clear objective on the agenda. An Office of the State Minister for European and Euro-Atlantic Integration was set up, responsible for inter-agency coordination on developing cooperation with the EU (and NATO). Simultaneously, bold statements were made by high-ranking Georgian officials. For example, then-president Mikheil Saakashvili directly proclaimed that Georgia would gain full membership of the EU during the next presidential term (2009-2013) (Gegeshidze 2006, 10). Additionally, all government institutions began flying the European Flag. It should be noted that during the process of developing the ENP Action Plan, Georgia insisted that the perspective of full membership be included in the preamble of the document. Even though this attempt was futile, full EU membership, unlike in previous times, was no longer a wish but rather a clearly outlined ambition. Such an ambition was supported by the increased pro-European sentiments among the Georgian public. The ENP intended to transform Georgia in terms of political, legal, and administrative frameworks to reach European standards. However, there was no provision of potential membership, a fact which was not met positively in Tbilisi. Therefore, there were often clashes between Georgian policies and the reform agenda within the ENP Action Plan (Gogolashvili 2017, 11). Ultimately, this resulted in Georgia lagging behind Ukraine and Moldova in terms of depth and pace of reforms.

The AA is the foremost vehicle of advancing Georgia's path to Europe. It is expected that the AA will bring about a number of advantages for Georgia, including: (a) stabilization of its economic and legal system, thus making it more predictable for investors and more business-friendly; (b) alignment of economic laws to those in the EU which will broaden the market for Georgian products and services; (c) better implementation of laws. Political cooperation between Tbilisi and Brussels is at a very high level. Many analyses have proven that the regulations governing co-operation between the two in the fields of foreign policy, security and defense which the AA sets out are as strong as those mentioned in association agreements signed with other partner countries (many of which are already members), and many aspects of co-operation are written in great detail and depth (Gogolashvili 2014, 7).

After the 2008 war with Russia, Georgia's prospects for real rapprochement with the EU became more prominent, most notably in areas such as free trade, a simplified visa regime and EU association—issues which had already been mentioned in the first communication[xiv] defining the EaP as one of its main tools for bilateral co-operation.

EU support to Georgia aims at improving the quality of life of ordinary Georgians in a tangible and visible manner and provides over € 120 million to Georgia annually in grant assistance. In this context, EU assistance to Georgia supports the country's reform efforts in line with the AA /DCFTA. EU support is funded through the European Neighbourhood Instrument (ENI) for the period 2014-2020. It replaced the European Neighbourhood and Partnership Instrument (ENPI) of 2007-2013 (Emerson and Kovrziridze 2016, 181). Georgia will continue to be one of the six countries benefiting from regional programs that support the EaP. According to the European External Action Service (EEAS) and the Commission's multi-annual indicative program for the Eastern neighborhood 2021-2027, these programs will amount to €632.24 million for 2021-2024. Assuming appropriations would remain the same for the three remaining years, it would mean a total regional envelope of €1 106 million for 2021-2027, an increase when compared with the €906 million under the ENI for 2014-2020. It should be noted that the ENP multi-annual indicative program now also foresees an extra allocation of € 929.88 million to support the deployment of budgetary guarantees in the Eastern neighborhood, through the EFSD+ or through MFA (Madatali and Jansen 2022, 16).

On 3 March 2022, Georgia presented its application for EU membership. On 17 June 2022, the European Commission presented its Opinions on the application for EU membership submitted by Ukraine, Georgia and the Republic of Moldova. Based on the Commission's opinion on the country's application for EU membership, Georgia's bid for a candidate status was rejected, instead it received a so-called membership perspective. Candidate status will be granted only, if Georgia addresses some key priorities. The Commission will monitor progress in fulfilling these priorities and report on them, as part of its regular enlargement package.[xv]

Unlike Georgia, Ukraine and Moldova received candidate status. The acceptance of Ukraine's membership application was granted by the EU as an encouragement, but unlike Georgia, Ukraine has problems related to corruption and crime control and prevention, rule of law, etc, but the situation has been changed a lot after the war. According to the data on the level of corruption, Ukraine was at a lower level than Georgia.[xvi] The rejection of Georgia's application can be explained by the Russian-Ukrainian war. First, after the start of the war, the West and the EU began to impose sanctions against Russia, expecting a similar response from Georgia as well, but it did not happen. Georgia only partially joined the sanctions imposed by the West and the EU, did not take serious steps and did not impose new sanctions. Therefore, it means that the EU "punished" Georgia. On the other hand, Georgian-South Ossetian and Georgian-Abkhazian conflicts remained frozen. It seems that the Russian-Ukrainian war is a good opportunity to intensify conflicts and open a second military front for Russia, but Georgia is not in a hurry to take any steps and aggravate relations with Russia, because it sees the disastrous situation of Ukraine. On the other hand no matter how much Russia is stuck on the first front, they will have time to support Abkhazia and South Ossetia. In addition, the Abkhazians and Ossetians will not only wait for Russia's response, but they will also counterattack Georgia, because they also welcomed Russia's decision to recognize the independence of Donetsk and Luhansk. Also, the Russian military continues to deploy its army in Abkhazia and Tskhinvali. Georgia's restraint is also due to the wish of receiving EU membership. If the conflict flares up again, the EU will not accept

Georgia's membership application until the problem is resolved, because the EU does not need any additional "headaches".

How Should the EU Respond to these Challenges?

Armenian and Georgian Cases

One way in which the EU demonstrates support to the South Caucasus countries is by strengthening the inter-parliamentary dimension. The platform of parliamentary cooperation between the EaP countries and the EU is the Euronest Parliamentary Assembly. It is the inter-parliamentary forum in which members of the European Parliament and the national parliaments of Ukraine, Moldova, Armenia, Azerbaijan and Georgia participate and forge closer political and economic ties with the EU. The Armenian side welcomed the idea of Euronest and inter-parliamentary cooperation within the framework of the EaP. Bilateral Armenia-EU inter-parliamentary cooperation takes place within the framework of the Parliamentary Cooperation Committee which gives the two sides an opportunity to exchange views and to make proposals on issues of common interest. For Armenia, Euronest and the Parliamentary Cooperation Committee are a great opportunity to gain experience in European parliamentarism. Armenia has been successfully integrated into the committee work of Euronest in a short period of time (Committee on Political Affairs, Human Rights and Democracy-POL, Committee on Economic Integration, Legal Approximation and Convergence with EU Policies-ECON, Committee on Energy Security-ENER, Committee on Social Affairs, Employment, Education, Culture and Civil Society-SOC. Armenia is thus actively working with the support of the EU, through which public interest in the EaP and in particular its parliamentary format is increasing.

The implementation of CEPA should become a guide to lead to stronger perspectives for Armenia. The EU supports its reform agenda by pursuing the implementation of CEPA; it appreciates Armenia's commitment to full implementation despite the current challenges that Armenia is facing.

The EU assists in overcoming the Covid pandemic, not only in Armenia but also Georgia. The EU, in cooperation with the World Health Organization, has provided medical equipment, PCR tests, personal protective equipment, and other relevant equipment to EaP countries to address health problems [EaP 2021, n. p.]. Through the EaP Solidarity Program, civil society grants were provided to local schools to organize distance learning and promote independent journalism and observation initiatives.[xvii] Within the framework of supporting small and medium-sized enterprises in Armenia and Georgia the EU implements the EU4Business program in three areas: business crisis support services, access to finance and better governance.[xviii] This makes it easy to take advantage of local currency loans, apply for grants during the crisis, and then develop the business. The EU provides assistance and opportunities to women [EU 2021, n. p.]. With this, they are able to break stereotypes and help local communities to overcome difficult situations. Support includes women-led businesses providing grants, loans, quality education, and promoting a fairer society. But people require more proactive engagement from the EU institutions, to improve consciousness to the common people about Western societies and to clarify how Europeans participate in the governing process in everyday life there. By using different programs, the EU should support practical and theoretical education of people in big cities, small towns and villages to understand the meaning of representative democracy, its essence and ideas. It is important for them to know how much that knowledge will give them for their practical, everyday life. Many people in Georgia understand very poorly what European-style democracy means and how many gains it brings for the improvement of society. That is why the EU should have an educational role, to share the European countries' experience of power transitions, balance of power between political center and regions, political pluralism and multiparty system and the menace of power consolidation in the hands of a sole political party across the country. Unfortunately, as it was common in the communist system, most of Georgian people currently consider that one political party to have authority at each level of government in a state. So, educating people even superficially in most regions will at least partly solve the constant governance problems and crisis there. As for the economic improvement, Georgia needs strong support in specific fields of the economy. For instance, the areas where Georgia requires Western support are improvement of transportation and other infrastructure, knowledge of business and trade principles, improved knowledge of EU regulations (especially for representatives of small businesses), and development of cooperatives. To bring Georgia's economy closer to the EU, medium and small businesses in particular need informational and educational assistance. It is not only the local challenge of the country but regional and global challenges as well because passive behavior of the EU will create a comfortable space for big powers, to exploit the local economic environment. So, Georgian small- and medium-sized businesses and farmers should see the EU market as more attractive to integrate with the West and decrease the dependency on Russia and China.

The judicial system and independence of the judiciary are among the most serious troubles for Georgia nowadays. The situation is complicated because most judges depend on one another and hesitate to harm each other. That is the reason why none of them admits that there are real problems inside the courts. But as we considered several controversial cases above, it is clear that the judicial system faces real challenges. In response to these controversies, the EU had already cut a macro-financial loan to Georgia which was a very palpable message to the Georgian people. When we take into consideration how civil society and common people try to handle a possible oppression from different branches of government, we should admit that sometimes they need tough reaction by the partners towards the ruling elite, because, as we know, when financial and political consolidation is too high on the one side, another part of society becomes vulnerable and needs a firm foreign support. So, the EU should continue sending distinct messages about what they dislike in the Georgian government and the ruling elite.

As for civil society in Armenia, it is at the center of attention of the EU. Relations of European bilateral and multilateral donors with Armenian society have been conducted mainly through the government. These contacts with Armenia have generally focused on building strong relations with representatives of the state's elite through the involvement of non-governmental actors (Raik 2006, 21). This changed with the launch of the ENP, in particular the EaP, as a result of which contacts between the civil society of the Republic of Armenia and the EU member states began to develop. The road to the formation and development of civil society has been difficult, full of failures and successes. At that time the number of civil society organisations, mainly non-governmental organisations (NGOs) reached about 5000, but civil society was fragmented, most of it existed only on paper (Paturyan et al. 2014, 263). The formal civil society sector is made up of one large group of so-called pocket NGOs organized by governmental groups or persons (Gevorgyan 2017, 10). These organizations leave few, if any, reasons for assessing their impact. The motivations for continuous maintenance of such organizations range from cultivating negative public perceptions to politicizing and, eventually, monopolizing the civil society sector (similar to the private sector), as one of the tools to sustain the regime. This initially created an unhealthy atmosphere and distrust towards civil society organizations, which changed in recent years as the EU began to focus on Armenian civil society. The issue of civil society was still addressed by the EU in the PCA signed in 1996, with an interest in engaging in the development of civil society in Armenia. Article 68 PCA states that "the parties shall encourage contacts and exchanges between their national, regional and judicial authorities […] and non-governmental organisations".[xix] With the support of ENI, the EU seeks to strengthen the capacity of civil society organizations to guarantee effective domestic accountability and local ownership and to play a full role in the democratization process. One of the EU programs to support civil society organizations in Armenia is the European Instrument for Democracy and Human Rights Program (EIDHR) which launched its activities in support of NGOs in Armenia. The main objective of EIDHR is to promote human rights and support Armenia in the areas of democratization, conflict prevention, and resolution. In 2003, for example, this Instrument funded 11 projects.[xx] Projects covered areas, such as the fight against corruption, peace building between Armenia and Azerbaijan, human rights protection, etc. The number of funded projects under EIDHR increased to 15 in 2010 and 12 in 2012. Some of the projects are long-term, such as for example establishing a one-year MA Program in Human Rights and Democratization at the Center of the European Studies of Yerevan State University for students coming from Armenia, Belarus, Ukraine, and Moldova (Yeritsyan 2016, 193). Besides, three new EU-funded projects focused on improving labor and social rights in Armenia were launched on 11 June 2021. The three projects are funded under the EIDHR. The total EU contribution amounts to € 1.138 million. The projects will be implemented by three civil society consortia led by OxYGen, Helsinki Citizens Assembly Vanadzor, and the Union of ICT Employers. Within these consortia 14 civil society organizations from across Armenia will be involved the projects activities.[xxi]

The EU is also trying to play a positive political role in the settlement of the Nagorno-Karabakh conflict. First of all, by expressing its support to the OSCE Minsk Group, it is trying to call for an end to Azerbaijan's aggression in Nagorno-Karabakh, as well as on the Armenian-Azerbaijani border. On 6 April 2022 a trilateral meeting took place between the Prime Minister of the Republic of Armenia Nikol Pashinyan and the President of Azerbaijan, Ilham Aliyev, and the President of the European Council, Charles Michel. As a result of the meetings a bilateral commission on the delimitation of the Armenian-Azerbaijan border will be established, which will have the authority to ensure security and stability along the border.[xxii]

The EU wants to establish stability and peace in the South Caucasus for the benefit of the people of the region, as there are other external actors in the South Caucasus that pursue differently, conflicting interests. Therefore, regional security and stability depend not only on these countries but also on external actors. This is why the conflicts in the South Caucasus are resolved not by negotiations, but by military means. Other foreign actors, including the Russian Federation and Türkiye, use the Armenian-Azerbaijani conflict as a means of maintaining their influence—Russia's influence on Armenia, and Türkiye's influence on Azerbaijan. The vivid proof of this is that in 2020 as a result of the war, Russian peacekeepers were deployed in Artsakh, as well as in the territory of the Republic of Armenia. And throughout the war, Türkiye helped Azerbaijan by all possible means: military, political, informational, diplomatic, etc.—under the slogan of one nation, two states aiming to strengthen its position in the region, pursuing its own interests. No matter how hard the EU tries to act as an honest mediator, conflicts of interest are also an obstacle to effective EU policy.

Conclusion

Summarizing the approaches discussed in this chapter, Armenia and Georgia clearly have common challenges: democratization and institution-building initiatives, human rights and rule of law, legal and judicial, economic problems, civil society, conflicts and security. But these challenges are at different levels in both countries, making the states unique cases. Georgia is one step ahead of Armenia in overcoming its challenges, that is why the EU's response to these challenges is different for two states. The development path of EU-Armenia and EU-Georgia relations and the expectations of Armenia and Georgia from the EU are also important. Georgia's goal is to become a member of the EU, and Armenia is aimed at keeping relations with the EU, taking into account its membership in the EAEU.

If the EU tries to play an active role in the settlement and resolution of conflicts, taking into account that there are other parties and actors besides the Armenia-EU and Georgia-EU parties, then other challenges will directly concern the given states and the EU. In order to overcome these challenges, the following proposals are distinguished according to Georgia and Armenia:

More specifically, to reach success in problematic issues, better public participation, awareness-raising, better knowledge and understanding of the EU in Armenia, particularly among civil society organizations, are needed. CEPA should be a stimulus for the development of civil society. The parties shall: (a) ensure involvement of civil society in relations between the EU and the Republic of Armenia; (b) enhance civil society participation in the public decision-making process, in particular by establishing an open, transparent and regular dialogue between, on the one hand, public institutions and, on the other, representative associations and civil society; (c) facilitate the process of institution-building and the consolidation of civil society in various ways, including inter alia: advocacy support, informal and formal networking, mutual visits and workshops, in particular with a view to improving the legal framework for civil society; and (d) enable civil-society representatives from each side to become acquainted with the processes of consultation and dialogue between civil and social partners on the other side, in particular with a view to further integrating civil society into the public policy-making process in the Republic of

Armenia. As a result, a political consciousness will be formed, contributing to citizens' awareness-raising, which will positively impact the election and political participation processes in general.

The European Commission recommends that Georgia be granted candidate status once Georgia fulfills the 12 priorities.[xxiii] At the same time, to handle the major challenges in Georgia the parties shall: (a) increase cooperation to create better basis for constant communication to the people in cities, also in regional settlements, including small towns and villages; (b) increase awareness for the people about local governance, meaning of multiparty system, perils of power consolidation and importance of power transitions between different political parties; (c) create practical and theoretical programs for local small/medium farmers and entrepreneurs to study specifics of European regulations and to choose the European market over autocratic and unstable countries; (d) call Georgian civil society and governmental structures to implement more regional cooperation frames between EaP countries that will guarantee the settlement of problems locally and maintain a stable environment on the regional level.

Bibliography

Cornell, Svante and Frederick Starr. 2006. *The Caucasus: A Challenge for Europe*. Central Asia-Caucasus Institute. Silk Road Program: 1-85.

Council of Europe. 2019. "Georgia—Support to the Implementation of the Judicial Reform." https://www.coe.int/en/web/cdcj/co-operationprojects/judicialreform-georgia.

Delcour, Laure and Kataryna Wolczuk. 2015 "The EU's Unexpected "Ideal Neighbour"? The Perplexing Case of Armenia's Europeanisation'". *Journal of European Integration* 37 (4): 491-507.

Dragneva, Rilka and Kataryna Wolczuk. 2017. "The Eurasian Economic Union: Deals, Rules and the Exercise of Power." Chatham House, The Royal Institute of International Affairs 1-25.

Emerson, Michael and Tamara Kovziridze. 2016. "Deepening EU- Georgian Relations: What, Why and How?". CEPS Research Paper: 1-201.

"EU launches #strongerwomen campaign in the Eastern partner countries". 2021, https://www.euneighbours.eu/en/east/stay-informed/news/eu-launches-strongerwomen-campaign-eastern-partner-countries.

"European Union Solidarity for Health Initiative in the Eastern Partnership Countries". 2021, https://www.euneighbours.eu/en/east/stay-informed/projects/european-union-solidarity-health-initiative-eastern-partnership/.

Gegeshidze, Archil. 2006. "Georgia in the Wider Europe Context: Bridging Divergent Interpretations". CPC International Fellowship Program, Open Society Institute: 1-49.

Gevorgyan, Valentina. 2017. "The Next Step in the Development of Armenian Civil Society." Open Society Foundations—Armenia: 1-27.

Ghazaryan, Narine and Laure Delcour. 2018. "From EU Integration Process to the Eurasian Economic Union: The Case of Armenia." In *Post-Soviet Constitutions and Challenges of Regional Integration: Adapting to European and Eurasian Integration Projects*, edited by P. Van Elsuwege and R. Petrov, 1-22. New York, Routledge.

Giragosian, Richard and Hrant Kostanyan. 2017. "EU-Armenian Relations: Charting a Fresh Course." CEPS Research Report 14: 1-30.

Gogolashvili, Kakha. 2014. "European Union-Georgia Political Association: Scope and Ambition." Opinion Paper No. 26, Georgian Foundation for Strategic and International Studies (GFSIS).

International Election Observatory Mission. 2021. Georgia—Local Elections, 2nd Round. OSCE, ODIHR. https://www.osce.org/odihr/elections/georgia/496309.

Joint Declaration of the Prague Eastern Partnership Summit, Prague, 7 May 2009, Brussels, 8435/09 (Presse 78): 6-11.

Khovorostyankina, Anna. 2017. "Constitutional Identity in the Context of Post-Soviet Transformation, Europeanization and Regional Integration Processes: the case of Armenia." *Armenian Journal of Political Science* 1 (6): 45-80.

Khovorostyankina, Anna. 2017. "EU-Armenia Comprehensive and Enhanced Partnership Agreement: What Does It Mean for Armenian Legal System?" *Armenian Journal of Political Science* 2 (7): 5-30.

Lynch, Dov. 2003. "The EU: Towards a Strategy." In *The South Caucasus: A Challenge for the EU*, edited by Dov Lynch, 171-192. Paris, *Chaillot Paper* 65: EU Institute for Security Studies.

Madatali, Ahamad and Talander Janset. 2022. "Association Agreement between the EU and Georgia." European Parliamentary Research Service: 1-76.

Mkrtchyan, Huseynov and Kakha Gogolashvili. 2009. "The European Union and the South Caucasus, Three Perspectives on the Future of the European Project from the Caucasus." Europe in Dialogue 01. Bielefeld.

National Statistics Office of Georgia. 2021. n.d. "Exports by Country." https://www.geostat.ge/en/modules/categories/637/export.

National Statistics Office of Georgia. 2021. n.d. "Imports by Country." https://www.geostat.ge/en/modules/categories/766/international-trade-in-services.

Paturyan, Yevgenya, Valentina Gevorgyan and Mariam Matevosyan. 2014. "Is 'Googling' a Technique? What the Internet Can Tell Us about the Non-Governmental Sector in Armenia." *Haigazian Armenological Review* 34: 257–267.

Prime Minister of the Republic of Armenia. 2022. https://www.primeminister.am/en/foreign-visits/item/2022/04/05/Nikol-Pashinyan-visit-to-Brussels/.

Raik, Kristi. 2006. "How to Step up the EU's Policy towards the Eastern Neighbourhood." CEPS Working Document 237: 1-37.

Rakopyan, Marina. 2020. "Human Rights and Democratisation during 2019: The Case of Armenia, Georgia and Moldova." *Global Campus Human Rights Journal* 4: 539-556.

Simão, Licínia. 2011. "EU-South Caucasus Relations: Do Good Governance and Security Go Together?" *Political Perspective* 5 (2): 33-57.

Terzyan, Aram. 2015. "Armenia's Foreign Policy between European Identity and Eurasian Integration." Eastern ChessBoard. Geopolitical Determinants and Challenges in Eastern Europe and the South Caucasus 88: 247-258.

Terzyan, Aram. 2016. "The Evolution of Armenia's Foreign Policy Identity: The Conception of Identity Driven Paths. Friends and Foes in Armenian Foreign Policy Discourse." In Values and Identity as Sources of Foreign Policy in Armenia and Georgia, edited by Kornely Kakachia and Alexander Markarov: 145-183. Tbilisi, Universal.

Waal De, Thomas. 2021. "The Nagorny Karabakh Conflict in its Fourth Decade." CEPS Working Document 2: 1-19.

Yeritsyan, Grigor. 2016. "The Role of the EU in the Development of the Civil Society in Armenia." *Civic Education and Democratization in the Eastern Partnership Countries* 16 (97): 189-206.

Zedelashvili, Davit. 2021. "*The Rule of Law in Georgia: What Can the EU Leverage?*". *VerfBlog*, https://verfassungsblog.de/rule-of-law-georgia/.

CHALLENGES OF EUROPEAN INTEGRATION   121

i   EU- Armenia relations, https://www.consilium.europa.eu/media/44397/685-an nex-5-a-armenia-factsheet.pdf.
ii   Transparency International, https://www.transparency.am/hy/media/statements/article/3121.
iii   Application of the International Convention on the Elimination of All Forms of Racial Discrimination (Armenia v. Azerbaijan), https://www.icj-cij.org/sites/default/files/case-related/180/180-20230222-ORD-01-00-EN.pdf.
iv   Aliyev: Azerbejian Pressing Ahead with Zangezur Corridor Construction, https://hetq.am/en/article/151219.
v   Comprehensive and Enhanced Partnership Agreement between the European Union and Armenia (CEPA), 2018. https://eeas.europa.eu/cepa-agreement-en_az.
vi   EU-Armenia Partnership Council, 18 May 2022, https://www.eeas.europa.eu/delegations/armenia/%C2%A0eu-armenia-partnership-council-18-may-2022_en?s=216.
vii   Ministry of Justice of the Republic of Armenia, https://moj.am/article/3207
viii NATO-Georgia relations, https://www.nato.int/nato_static_fl2014/assets/pdf/pdf_2019_10/191002_Media_Backgrounder_Georgia_en.pdf.
ix   Georgia, Freedom House, https://freedomhouse.org/country/georgia/freedom-world/2022.
x   European Commission. 2016. "EU-Georgia Deep and Comprehensive Free Trade Area".
xi   EU Says Georgia Failed Court Reform Condition, https://civil.ge/archives/437968.
xii   President Zurabishvili Pardons Gigi Ugulava, Irakli Okruashvili, https://civil.ge/archives/352010.
xiii MEPs Talk "Political Nature" of Saakashvili's Imprisonment, GD Lashes Back, https://civil.ge/archives/448997.
xiv   'Eastern Partnership', Communication from the Commission to the European Parliament and the Council COM(2008) 823 final, 3 December 2008, p. 4, available at [http://eur-lex.europa.eu/legalcontent/EN/TXT/PDF/?uri=CELEX:52008DC0823&from=EN].
xv   EU—Georgia Relations, https://neighbourhood-enlargement.ec.europa.eu/european-neighbourhood-policy/countries-region/georgia_en#eu--georgia-relations.
xvi   Transparency International Corruption Perceptions Index, https://www.transparency.org/en/cpi/2021/index/ukr.
xvii Eastern Partnership COVID-19 Solidarity Programme. 2021, https://www.euneighbours.eu/en/east/stay-informed/projects/eastern-partnership-covid-19-solidarity-programme.
xviii EU4Business, https://covid-19-armenia.eu4business.eu/en/.
xix   EU-Armenia Partnership and Cooperation Agreement. 1999, https://eeas.europa.eu/sites/eeas/files/euarmenia_partnership_and_cooperation_agreement_en.pdf.
xx   European Neighbourhood and Partnership Instrument: Armenia, https://www.deutscharmenischegesellschaft.de/wp-content/uploads/2010/04/EU-Komission-COUNTRY-STRATEGY-PAPER-2007-2013-Armenia.pdf.
xxi   EU-funded project to improve labour and social rights in Armenia, https://euneighbourseast.eu/news/latest-news/eu-funded-project-to-improve-labour-and-social-rights-in-armenia/.
xxii Pashinyan, Aliyev to meet in Brussels on April 6, https://hetq.am/en/article/142895.
xxiii Opinion on the EU membership application by Georgia, https://ec.europa.eu/commission/presscorner/detail/en/qanda_22_3800.

Hybrid War against European Political Integration of Armenia: A Dead End or a Springboard on the Way to the EU?

Ashot Aleksanyan

Abstract

This chapter analyzes the challenges stemming from hybrid warfare waged by Russia and Azerbaijan again Armenia. In this regard, the key dimensions of European integration of post-war Armenia are considered, accompanied by an analysis of security threats to the country's resilience as a state and actor in the South Caucasus. Armenia's revised role throughout the transformation of the regional security system in the South Caucasus stands out as a key factor in the further development of the EU-led geopolitical space. The issues studied comparatively are also relevant from the point of view of Armenia's European integration perspectives, as opposed to the fact that since the demise of the USSR Armenia has been under Russia's domination. While enhanced cooperation with the EU has the potential to improve Armenia's standing in the South Caucasus, it could also equip Yerevan with the tools to counter the Russian and Azerbaijani hybrid and destabilizing influence.

Keywords: Velvet Revolution; Armenian statehood; resilient transformation; Eastern Partnership; democratic transition; European Armenia

Introduction

After the collapse of the USSR, the South Caucasus region faced the challenge of re-establishing the system of bilateral and multilateral partnerships. Its complexity is explained by the presence of a neither-war-nor-peace situation, unresolved ethno-territorial conflicts and competition between various actors in the region, in particular the

United States of America, the Russian Federation, the European Union (EU), the Republic of Türkiye and the Islamic Republic of Iran. Directly adjacent to the South Caucasus region is the Russian North Caucasus as well as the Greater Middle East region, where complex domestic and international processes have been unfolding in recent years.

Most significant transport communications pass through the South Caucasus or could potentially pass through it. This includes foremostly oil and gas pipelines through which hydrocarbon fuels can be transported from the Caspian Basin and Central Asia to European and other world markets.

Since the demise of the USSR, Armenia's relations with its neighboring countries have been difficult and often conflicting. On the other hand, Armenia was able to establish strong ties both with the EU, Council of Europe, OSCE and NATO, as well as with the USA and Western states (Moore 2022; Wishnick 2022). The experience of recent decades shows that the foreign policy of Armenia, as a small state in size and potential, is utterly vulnerable to the geopolitical shifts in the region, especially since the Second Karabakh War in 2020. This issue is no less relevant from the point of view of the EU's interests in the South Caucasus, since Armenia signed the Armenia-EU Comprehensive and Enhanced Partnership Agreement (CEPA).[i]

After the Velvet Revolution and early parliamentary elections in 2018 and 2021, Nikol Pashinyan was appointed Prime Minister of Armenia and new approaches to political integration with the EU and the settlement of the Nagorno-Karabakh conflict emerged, both before and after the Second Karabakh War. It should be noted that there has been limited research in which a comparative analysis of hybrid war against post-war Armenia, as well as the role of post-war Armenia on the path to political integration with the EU and in the structure of international relations in the South Caucasus, has been discussed. Hence, the purpose of this paper is to present a comparative analysis of the role of post-war Armenia's political integration with the EU while struggling with the hybrid challenges stemming from both Russia and Azerbaijan.

This paper uses a number of political science approaches to analyze the system and structure of political and economic integration with the EU, as well as the process of formation and implementation of the foreign policy of the EaP countries (Libaridian 2023; Zięba 2023; Lonardo 2023; Lavrelashvili and Van Hecke 2023; Lucas and Lo 2022). Particular attention is paid to the neorealist paradigm, according to which the foreign policy of most EaP countries faces limitations arising from the emerging structure of interstate relations at the global and regional levels (Kennedy-Pipe and Zaidi 2021; Schatz 2023; Coyle 2021). Based on this view, the current state and prospects of relations between Armenia and the EU, as well as Armenia's relations with its neighbors and extra-regional actors also deserve scholars' attention (Vasilyan 2020; Topychkanov 2022).

A considerable number of scholarly works draws on a comparative analysis of the integration of Armenia and other EaP countries with the EU in their modern iterations (Muradov 2022; Tsygankov, Tsygankov and Gonzales 2023; Klimovich 2023; Pidkuimukha 2023). At the same time, the hybrid role of Russia as a traditional actor who closely observed what was happening in the South Caucasus remained insufficiently studied (Helfrich 2023; Anton 2024; Loftus 2023).

This chapter argues that after the Velvet Revolution of 2018 and the Second Karabakh War in 2020, the role of the authoritarian actors of the South Caucasus region (Iran, Turkey and Russia) increased, forming a hybrid mechanism aimed at limiting the European integration of Armenia. The current stage of European integration of postwar Armenia is characterized by an increased degree of uncertainty in international relations and structural changes in regional politics. This situation leads to complex, multifaceted processes and profound social and economic transformations. In conditions of regional instability, disruptions occur in the functioning of democratic mechanisms putting even the resilience of the EU to the test.

Democratic Transition of Armenia and Its Alignment with the EU

Armenia's Velvet Revolution of 2018 became the "boiling point" of the democratic transition of post-Soviet Armenia to European Armenia. Like all other post-Soviet states, Armenia was doomed to become a country with an oligarchic political system, albeit with certain differences, namely the perspective of European integration within the framework of the EaP and the Nagorno-Karabakh conflict becoming an important factors in the democratic transition of Armenia.

The November 2013 EU EaP summit was key for Armenia, as Russia exerted strong influence to prevent it from signing an Association Agreement (AA) with the EU (Rouet and Côme 2019; Slobodnikova, Terem and Gura 2019). This became a red line for Armenian CSOs and pro-European political parties which began to actively criticize the "one-person" decision of Armenian President Serzh Sargsyan.

Until 2013 and then after 2020, Armenia tried, in spite of serious pressure from Russia, to combine European integration and Eurasian rapprochement. The year 2013 was a turning point, and Russia significantly cut funding and changed its rhetoric towards Armenia, whereas the EU, even after Armenia refused to sign the AA, continued to support it. At the same time, Russia softened its rhetoric and generally strove to keep relations with Armenia at a fairly high level. The April 2016 war between Azerbaijan and Nagorno-Karabakh showed that in the conditions of the oligarchic political system of Armenia, Nagorno-Karabakh would be destined to military defeat, which ultimately led to the Velvet Revolution of 2018.

The emerging oligarchic authoritarian system was in deep contradiction to the commitment of the Armenian people to democratic values and the need to ensure the national security of Armenia in the long term. As a result, a significant part of the Armenian population left the country, realizing the fundamental injustice of the emerging political system and its inability to solve the problems of ensuring national security. These trends reached their peak by 2016, when, thanks to the supply of offensive weapons and military equipment to Azerbaijan by Russia and Israel, the military balance was upset which provoked Azerbaijan to once again launch large-scale military operations.

In 2018, the growth of crisis tendencies in the political system of Armenia took on the most acute, but at the same time structured forms. At the climax of the crisis, an event occurred that was called, within civil and political discourse, the Velvet Revolution. This phenomenon became possible due to the uniqueness of the Armenian political system, coupled with a large number of unresolved social and economic problems (Antonyan 2023), the lack of a unified ideological concept among the leaders of the ruling Republican Party of Armenia and parliamentary parties, as well as the intense influence of external factors on the development of the Armenian political crisis.

The Velvet Revolution and the Strengthening of the European Integration Agenda

The starting point of the national uprising leading to the Velvet Revolution was the violation of the social contract concluded between President Serzh Sargsyan and the Armenian society in 2015 during the adoption of the new Constitution and the transition to a parliamentary form of government. Understanding all the threats of the transition to a parliamentary system in conditions of war and the immaturity of political parties, society agreed to adopt a new Constitution on the condition that Serzh Sargsyan would not aspire to occupy the post of the first person of the state for the third time. Yet, by running for a third term, Serzh Sargsyan sharply escalated the situation in Armenia. Moreover, isolation from society led to the fact that already during the process of appointment to the post of Prime Minister, Serzh Sargsyan allowed himself a number of statements which crossed a "red line". Society saw in Serzh Sargsyan's words a threat of repeating the scenario of March 1, 2008, when protesters were shot on the streets of Yerevan and blood was shed.

The political opposition action "Take a step and reject Serge!", which was unfolding by this time, led by Nikol Pashinyan, largely independently of the leader himself, began to change its status due to the radicalization of society (Ohanyan 2021). Having started the action in one of the Armenian cities as an opposition leader, Nikol Pashinyan entered Yerevan, ready to revolt, in a different capacity and, to his credit, was ready to accept a new role and lead an uprising aimed at overthrowing Serzh Sargsyan and the ruling Republican Party of Armenia. By mid-April, the protests had acquired an all-Armenian scale, and Nikol Pashinyan received the mandate of a national leader called upon to carry out political transition and dismantle the oligarchic authoritarian political system in Armenia. The taboo on the shedding of blood left its mark on the uprising, which acquired a non-violent, bloodless character in compliance with the principle of the rule of law. A distinctive style and handwriting of the Armenian Velvet Revolution was formed, the first stage of which ended with the resignation of Serzh Sargsyan and the appointment of Nikol Pashinyan as Prime Minister.

The next stage of political transition was the holding of early parliamentary elections. Attempts at revenge on the part of the political forces of the old regime led to a sharp and unequivocal rebuff from society and an understanding of the need to go as quickly as possible to early parliamentary elections, which took place in December 2018. And if in the first stages of the Velvet Revolution Nikol Pashinyan's appeal to the rule of law and nonviolent methods of struggle were perceived as an approach slowing down the revolutionary process, the events of the fall of 2018 showed that this was a justified step (Derluguian and Hovhannisyan 2022).

The chosen strategy makes it extremely difficult for the opposition from the losing oligarchic system, which is not accustomed to operating with non-violent methods and within the framework of public forms of political struggle. Moreover, the attempt at counter-revolutionary revenge in early October 2018 showed that appealing to the rule of law accustoms society to non-violent methods of struggle and helps strengthen the corresponding political culture, which in itself is an important achievement of the Velvet Revolution.

The support of the Armenian people is the main and today practically the only factor allowing Nikol Pashinyan to maintain power. The direct mandate of the people, as an awakened sovereign, makes the task of neutralizing Nikol Pashinyan extremely difficult by the previous regime. The leader's intention to give society the functions of controlling political transitions based on the principle of the rule of law and non-violent methods raises the level of political self-awareness of society, creating the preconditions for holding early elections and moving to the next stage of the Velvet Revolution.

The Future of "Velvet Integration"

The Republic of Armenia entered 2019, completing the transition from executive to parliamentary power, thereby initiating similar processes in Nagorno-Karabakh. However, the Armenian people quickly came to the understanding that simultaneous revolutionary changes in both Armenian states were extremely risky, given the state of war. A situation could arise where the intensification of an external conflict in conditions of internal political instability would lead to loss of control, chaos and ultimately defeat. A consensus was reached among the Armenian people that the process of transition of power in the Republic of Armenia and Nagorno-Karabakh should be spaced out over time. Moreover, after the end of the transition of power in Armenia, it seemed to become possible to carry out a similar process in Nagorno-Karabakh not by revolutionary methods, but in a softer form of transformation, when a change of power occurs in a controlled form without the need for using street fighting methods. It was hoped that in the time remaining before the next presidential and parliamentary elections, the society of Nagorno-Karabakh would nominate public figures from their midst who were capable of carrying out systemic reforms.

Along with the initiation of democratic reforms and European integration of Armenia, the new government had to begin to develop and implement systemic reforms (Khvorostiankina 2021). This task was complicated by the fact that the Velvet Revolution was in many ways unexpected for its organizers. Indeed, there were no analogues in world political history on which to rely (Ohanyan 2021) and no precedents for systemic reform in the face of an active military threat in a dynamic security environment (Avdaliani 2022; Simão 2018; Maass 2019).

The War to Isolate Armenia: Managing Enmity and the Ally's Military Trap

After the Velvet Revolution in Armenia and after early parliamentary elections in October 2018, Nikol Pashinyan was appointed Prime Minister of Armenia. After Pashinyan's appointment, new approaches emerged around the process of resolving the Nagorno-Karabakh conflict. Armenia demonstrated its readiness to regulate relations with Azerbaijan and Turkey, as well as to return to the democratic format of negotiations around Nagorno-Karabakh. According to Pashinyan, Nagorno-Karabakh should be a full-fledged party in the negotiations on the Karabakh conflict, since Pashinyan himself represents only

Armenia and the Armenian people, and cannot in any way be a representative of Nagorno-Karabakh whose population does not participate in the Armenian elections.

The Azerbaijani side was against the participation of the Nagorno-Karabakh authorities in negotiations on a democratic settlement of the conflict, although the participation of all parties in the negotiations could have had a very constructive result. Regarding possible compromises and the possible transfer of 7 regions to Azerbaijan, Pashinyan clarified after his appointment that compromises can be discussed only when Azerbaijan gives a signal that it is ready to accept the existential right and security of the population of Nagorno-Karabakh. It is worth noting that the return of 7 regions and the security in Nagorno-Karabakh was supposed to minimize new risks and resolve deadlock situations. At various stages of negotiations, the presidents of Armenia, with the assistance of Russia, agreed to the return of 7 regions to Azerbaijan, in exchange for official recognition of independent status. However, the most important progress in the approach to resolving the Nagorno-Karabakh conflict was Pashinyan's statement at the Munich Security Conference on February 15, 2020. During the discussion around the Nagorno-Karabakh conflict, Pashinyan stated that any solution to the Nagorno-Karabakh conflict must be acceptable to the people of Armenia, the people of Karabakh and the people of Azerbaijan. In fact, Pashinyan is the only leader of Armenia who noted the need for a solution to the conflict to be accepted by the Azerbaijani people.

Nevertheless, Armenia found itself trapped by Russia as its military ally, since the military presence of Russia on the territory of Armenia and the degree of dependence of the security systems between Armenia and Russia offered ample opportunities to isolate Armenia from European integration (Petraitis 2021; Tsybulenko and Kajander 2021; Marsili 2021; Usov 2023). The first stage of the Russian hybrid war was the Second Karabakh War from September to November 2020. The second stage of the Russian hybrid war was the so-called Russian peacekeeping mission which lasted until the end of September 2023. Proof of the hybridity of the Russian peacekeeping contingent was the fact that in the zone of their responsibility the Azerbaijani army launched a military operation in Nagorno-Karabakh under the pretext of a so-called anti-terrorism measure, thereby completely clearing Nagorno-Karabakh of its ethnic Armenian population. The third stage of the Russian hybrid war began on 17 April 2024 with the withdrawal of the Russian peacekeeping contingent from Nagorno-Karabakh (Politico 2024). Russia is withdrawing its so-called peacekeepers from Nagorno-Karabakh despite the fact that they were supposed to remain in the region for at least five years. The official explanation for this was that Russia no longer sees the point of having so-called peacekeepers on the territory of Nagorno-Karabakh after the forced resettlement of the Armenian population. But in fact, the main reason for the decision on the early withdrawal of the contingent was that they failed to spark a new war between Armenia and Azerbaijan, and also failed to resolve the issue of Armenia's security.

One of the reasons that Azerbaijan started the Second Karabakh War in 2020 was precisely Russia's desire to isolate Armenia, as well as Azerbaijan itself, from European integration (Davidzon 2022). Ironically, its lack of willingness to contribute to the resolution of the post-war Karabakh conflict since the end of 2020 contributed to Armenia's turn to the West in search of support and assistance. The Kremlin manipulated the "enmity / hostility" between Armenia and Azerbaijan, while for the president of Azerbaijan, with the support of Turkey and Russia, a large-scale war against the small Nagorno-Karabakh and Armenia, guaranteed the long-awaited victory and increase in prestige and respect for Aliyev. Due to increased mistrust and clashes between Russia and the West, the OSCE Minsk Group was actually unable to continue the process of negotiations to resolve the Karabakh conflict within the framework of the principles of international law.

Russia's support for Azerbaijan led to the fact that deliberately accusing Armenia of "strengthening military positions," Azerbaijan launched the so-called anti-terrorist operation of a local nature in Nagorno-Karabakh. For the Armenian population of Nagorno-Karabakh and the political leadership of Armenia, the new military actions in the region came as a shock and were met with accusations of Azerbaijan's attempts to unleash another large-scale aggression against the people of Nagorno-Karabakh to complete the policy of ethnic cleansing. As expected, the reaction of the so-called Russian peacekeepers was inaction, which led to the forced relocation of more than 120,000 people from Nagorno-Karabakh to Armenia.

Even after September 2023, when Nagorno-Karabakh and its public institutions and organizations *de facto* ceased to exist, the militarization of the South Caucasus and the threat of a new war against Armenia continued. It is obvious that Russia's main goal is to isolate the region from the EU through Azerbaijani authoritarian leadership, thereby continuing its aggression against Armenia.

At the moment, as Armenia presents its "Crossroads of Peace" project,[ii] it is more difficult for Azerbaijan, Russia and Turkey to come to a compromise. If for Armenia a peace agreement with Azerbaijan and normalization of relations with Turkey is a guarantor of regional stability and European integration, for the authoritarian leadership of Azerbaijan and Russia a peace agreement with Armenia is considered a concession, criticized by the political elites of both countries and considered a sign of their weakness (Lebanidze 2020). In this context, the rights of life and security of the population of Nagorno-Karabakh are completely ignored which in the Azerbaijani-Russian deal directly sees risks for the security and physical existence of Nagorno-Karabakh.

Despite the enormous efforts of the EU, OSCE and Council of Europe, as well as the USA and France, Russia is nevertheless blocking, and during negotiations to resolve the Karabakh conflict, the positions of the parties collide, which, according to Azerbaijan, cannot be realized together. This is Azerbaijan's position on the territorial integrity of the country and Armenia's position on the right to life and security of the Armenian population of Nagorno-Karabakh.

The EU actively supports both the meetings of the leaders of Armenia and Azerbaijan, which are organized in the format of the summit of the European Political Community. It is also important that the EU organizes negotiations in a "two plus three" format with the participation of France, Germany and the EU. But despite this, Azerbaijani President Ilham Aliyev refused to participate in the meeting in Granada on October 5, 2023, without the participation of Turkey, which was attended by the leaders of Armenia, France, Germany, as well as the President of the European Council Charles Michel.

Military rhetoric, hate speech, propaganda and claims to the territorial integrity of Armenia also have a negative impact on the attitude of countries and the process of conflict resolution. Thus, at various Congresses of the ruling party New Azerbaijan, President Aliyev repeatedly stated that the capital Yerevan and some other regions of Armenia are historical Azerbaijani lands and Azerbaijan will do everything necessary to return them[iii]. Such propaganda contributes to the atmosphere of mistrust between the populations of the two countries, and also blocks the signing of a future Peace Treaty.

After 24 February 2022, when Russia started its so-called special military operation in Ukraine, the possible ways for a peaceful resolution of the Nagorno-Karabakh conflict and the participation of the Russian peacekeeping contingent in it were risky. Based on all said above, we can conclude that although the issue is very complex and multi-layered, it can still be resolved with the support of the EU and the West, as well as the sincere desire of the parties (Kocamaz 2022). For a peaceful solution to the conflict, it is necessary to eliminate aggressive military rhetoric and prepare the population of the two countries for compromise and peace. Resolution of the conflict is possible only after changes in the populations' views on the conflict, transformation of the mentality of societies and the creation of an atmosphere of trust. In the current situation, even with a great desire to resolve the conflict on the part of the EU and Western countries, the authorities of the conflicting countries cannot make compromises, since Russia risks losing the trust of the people and authorities (Yavuz and Gunter 2023; Babayev and Spanger 2020). Only after democratic transformation and diversification of the foreign policies of Armenia and Azerbaijan, as well as the views of the population, will it become possible to move on to constructive negotiations, which, as we see, should be based on the Peace Treaty, which considers the main positions of the countries regarding the conflict.

The new principles of the Peace Treaty must be fully finalized along with the mechanisms for their implementation, eliminating risks and uncertainties. In fact, the most difficult thing, in our opinion, is the transformation of the mentality of the population and the creation of an atmosphere of trust which is completely absent today. The new approach of Prime Minister of Armenia Nikol Pashinyan regarding the resolution of the conflict, which should be acceptable both to the people of Armenia, Karabakh, and the people of Azerbaijan, is a small step towards transforming society's views on the conflict. To achieve it, intractable conflicts theory may be consulted which implies many ways to change the perception of conflict on the part of societies through the efforts of CSOs, the role of the media in shaping the perception of the conflict, as well as its description in textbooks. In this context, it is necessary to note the role of the EU for the peaceful settlement of the Nagorno-Karabakh conflict, which, in fact, is aimed specifically at working with members of the societies involved in the conflict to change their perception and to create a peaceful atmosphere between them.

Addressing the Challenges of the Russian Hybrid War

Armenia has designed an effective anti-hybrid war strategy against Russia with the help of the EU and EU member states. In this context, the key event was on 6 October 2022 in Prague, on the sidelines of the first European Political Community when the President of Azerbaijan and the Prime Minister of Armenia signed a statement recognizing the Alma Ata 1991 Declaration (European Council 2022). An important step in post-war Armenia was that on 5 October 2023, Prime Minister of Armenia Nikol Pashinyan, with the support of the EU, signed the Declaration of Recognition of the Borders of Azerbaijan, which included Nagorno-Karabakh (European Council 2023). This happened after the conflict escalated in early autumn 2023, when Azerbaijan took control of Nagorno-Karabakh.

Residents of Nagorno-Karabakh were under blockade by Azerbaijan from December 2022 until the mass exodus at the end of September 2023. The Lachin corridor was closed even for humanitarian cargo until September 24, 2023. All this time, under the influence of Russia, the Azerbaijani Armed Forces launched a hybrid operation in Nagorno-Karabakh, one of the goals of which was to force the dissolution of all government bodies and the disbandment of the army. In all the mediations of the Russian peacekeepers, there was a desire to include Armenia in a new conflict, but the Armenian government appealed to the EU and EU members to reach an agreement on signing a peace treaty. After this, under the mediation of the so-called Russian peacekeepers, several rounds of hybrid negotiations between representatives of Azerbaijan and Nagorno-Karabakh took place, dedicated to issues of reintegration. On 24 September 2023, the Azerbaijani side opened the Lachin corridor, forced resettlement began and people began to leave Nagorno-Karabakh en masse and arrive in Armenia.

The core tool against Armenia's Russian hybrid war is the Armenian government's "Crossroads of Peace" project, which presupposes a constructive foreign policy for Armenia and aims to radically change the image of Armenia in the region (World Economic Forum 2024; Mission of the RA to the EU 2024). It is in the context of this project that the Pashinyan government is negotiating with Azerbaijan, thereby confirming its readiness to establish a stable and resilient peace in the region based on the sovereignty and independence of states, as well as mutual interest in diversifying regional infrastructures and transport channels. The project is an Armenian model of resilience with the goal of breaking out of isolation by becoming a logistics hub in the region after the 44-day war in 2020. It is important to note that the Pashinyan Government rejected the 'corridor logic' of Russia and Azerbaijan in unblocking communications, put forward by Azerbaijan, while recognizing the controlling function of Russia, whose peacekeeping contingent until September 2023 formally ensured the "non-movement" of the Lachin corridor. After the events that took place in Nagorno-Karabakh, including the illegal blockade of the Lachin corridor, the military aggression of Azerbaijan on 19 September 2023, the entire population of Nagorno-Karabakh was forcibly displaced from their country of permanent residence. All this once again showed the hybrid goals of Russia which tried, under the threat of aggression, to gain control over the transit communications of the Armenian territory. It can be argued that in the short and medium term the Armenian government managed to effectively block the hybrid challenges of Russia and Azerbaijan, thereby preventing any control by either party over the transit communications of its territory. This meant that Armenia had never agreed by any document to limit its sovereignty, and the control of a third country could not be established over any part of its sovereign territory. Perhaps this is why recently the political leadership of Armenia, speaking about negotiations with Azerbaijan, refers to the principles agreed upon in Brussels and then adopted in Granada through the mediation of the EU.

In the context of the effective struggle of the Armenian government, it is worth noting the fact that the EU established the EU Mission in Armenia (EUMA) in response to an official request from the Armenian authorities to station a full-fledged civilian EU mission on the Armenian-Azerbaijani border (EEAS 2023). On 20 March 2024, the Armenian Parliament ratified an agreement on the status of the EUMA on its border with Azerbaijan (NA of the RA 2024). This is another tool of the Pashinyan Government against the Russian hybrid war against post-war Armenia. This, on the one hand, minimizes the risk of a new war between Armenia and Azerbaijan, and also includes the EU in the process of maintaining the stability of peaceful coexistence. On the other hand, Russia's desire to increase its armed forces on the territory of Armenia, which is being shared under the pretext of supposedly containing Armenia, is restrained, but in fact this could become a new stage of military aggression and limiting the European integration of Armenia. It is in this context that one should understand the early withdrawal of the peacekeeping contingent from Nagorno-Karabakh and Russian steps to destabilize logistics communications in the region and with the West, that is, any new road for Armenia to the outside world and an economic opportunity for Armenia, and is a hybrid lever for Russia to control and isolate Armenian "Crossroads of Peace" project.

Conclusion

In light of the tectonic shifts taking place in the region throughout the last decade, Armenia has found itself at a crossroads, facing increased involvement from the EU and its readiness to contribute to strengthening the resilience of its domestic decision-making institutions as well as border monitoring. The window of opportunity to emerge as a pro-European actor in the South Caucasus, to distance itself from Russia's security umbrella and to resolve the long-lasting conflict with Azerbaijan offers Yerevan an unprecedented chance to reshape its posture in the region. The reform-minded political elite of the Velvet Revolution of 2018 was able to influence the mobilization of

Armenian society by calling towards common cultural and European values. At the same time, the delay of crucial decisions to be made will surely exert a negative impact on Armenia from geopolitical, economic, and humanitarian standpoints.

Considering the multi-layered nature and complexity of each of the challenges mentioned above, this chapter has shown that not a single theoretical standpoint could grasp the full picture, since the reasons for their genesis, historical, social and economic prerequisites, their course and negotiation processes differ.

While Armenia counted on Russia's and the CSTO's support as security guarantors in the region, the latter did not intend to adhere to any firm commitments, either during the Second Karabakh War in 2020 or in the post-war timeframe. When Azerbaijan unleashed another large-scale aggression against the people of Nagorno-Karabakh on 19 September 2023, the Russian peacekeeping contingent ignored the shelling of civilian settlements in Nagorno-Karabakh under the pretext of destroying military installations.

The peaceful resolution of the Nagorno-Karabakh conflict, although it has some constructive foundation, is still far from a complete resolution. Hence, the EU has the potential to exert a special role in the negotiation process, due to the bilateral cooperation with the stakeholders involved, and Russia facing increasing isolation due to its war in Ukraine. By acting as a guarantor of European integration and a mediator in the negotiation process in the post-war conflict in Nagorno-Karabakh, as well as with individual initiatives of trilateral negotiations, the EU has demonstrated its willingness to play a key role in resolving this conflict.

The devastating outcomes of the Second Karabakh War for Armenia, Azerbaijan's decisive stance to win the war and Russia's distancing have further contributed to Yerevan's decision to change the trajectory towards the EU as its key strategic partner. Nevertheless, dire economic and social conditions domestically, the disenchantment of Armenian society with the outcomes of the war, and the lack of effective response on behalf of Armenia have been deteriorating popular trust towards democratic institutions. The EU, considering the fragile position of Armenia after the Second Karabakh War, has been gradually turning to different formats of cooperation with Armenia,

Azerbaijan, and Türkiye with the view to ensure stability in the South Caucasus. Consequently, there is an opportunity for the EU to expand its political influence in the region by using its extensive networks of political and economic influence.

Bibliography

Aleksanyan, Ashot. 2020. "Civil Society as a Phenomenon of Post-Soviet Political Life: A Threat or a Guarantor of National Security?" *Transformation and Development: Studies in the Organization for Security and Cooperation in Europe (OSCE) Member States*, edited by Anja Mihr, 29-49. Cham: Springer.

Anton, Oleinik. 2024. Studying War Propaganda. In *A Comparative Analysis of Political and Media Discourses about Russia's Invasion of Ukraine*, edited by Oleinik Anton, 51-78. Palgrave Macmillan, Cham.

Antonyan, Yulia. 2023. "Power, Family and Business: Practices of Oligarchic Economy in Late Soviet and Post-Soviet Armenia (Before 2018)." In *Family Firms and Business Families in Cross-Cultural Perspective: Bringing Anthropology Back In*, edited by Tobias Koellner, 83-113. Palgrave Macmillan, Cham.

Avdaliani, Emil. 2022. "Russia's 'Return' to the South Caucasus." In *New World Order and Small Regions*, edited by Emil Avdaliani, 191-224. Singapore: Palgrave Macmillan.

Babayev, Azer, and Hans-Joachim Spanger. 2020. "A Way Out for Nagorno-Karabakh: Autonomy, Secession—or What Else?" In *The Nagorno-Karabakh Deadlock: Insights from Successful Conflict Settlements*, edited by Azer Babayev, Bruno Schoch, and Hans-Joachim Spanger, 277-320. Wiesbaden: Springer VS.

Biryukov, Oleksandr. 2023. "International Law and Frozen Conflicts in Eastern Europe and the Caucasus." In *International Law and Development in the Global South*, edited by Emeka Duruigbo, Remigius Chibueze, and Sunday Gozie Ogbodo, 79-98. Palgrave Macmillan, Cham.

Coyle, James J. 2021. "Diplomacy Surrounding Frozen Conflict." In *Russia's Interventions in Ethnic Conflicts*, edited by James J. Coyle, 115-164. Cham: Palgrave Macmillan.

Davidzon, Igor. 2022. "Regional Security Governance in Post-Soviet Eurasia—Summary and Conclusions." In *Regional Security Governance in Post-Soviet Eurasia: The History and Effectiveness of the Collective Security Treaty Organization*, edited by Igor Davidzon, 185-193. Cham: Palgrave Macmillan.

Derluguian, Georgi, and Ruben Hovhannisyan. 2022. "The Post-Soviet Revolution in Armenia: Victory, Defeat, and Possible Future." In *Handbook of Revolutions in the 21st Century. Societies and Political Orders in Transition*, edited by Jack A. Goldstone, Leonid Grinin, and Andrey Korotayev, 899-922. Cham: Springer.

EBRD. 2023. "Sustainable transport connections between Europe and Central Asia: Final Report." *June 16, 2023*. Accessed April 20, 2024. https://transport.ec.europa.eu/system/files/2023-06/Sustainable_transport_connections_between_Europe_and_Central_Asia.pdf.

EEAS. 2023. "EU Mission in Armenia (EUMA)." *February 28, 2023*. Accessed April 20, 2024. https://www.eeas.europa.eu/euma/eu-mission-armenia-euma_en.

European Commission. 2024. "Global Gateway: EU and Central Asian countries agree on building blocks to develop the Trans-Caspian Transport Corridor." *January 30, 2024*. Accessed April 20, 2024. https://international-partnerships.ec.europa.eu/news-and-events/news/global-gateway-eu-and-central-asian-countries-agree-building-blocks-develop-trans-caspian-transport-2024-01-30_en.

European Council. 2022. "Statement following quadrilateral meeting between President Aliyev, Prime Minister Pashinyan, President Macron and President Michel, 6 October 2022." *October 7, 2022*. Accessed April 20, 2024. https://www.consilium.europa.eu/en/press/press-releases/2022/10/07/statement-following-quadrilateral-meeting-between-president-aliyev-prime-minister-pashinyan-president-macron-and-president-michel-6-october-2022/.

European Council. 2023. "Statement by Prime Minister Nikol Pashinyan of Armenia, President Michel of the European Council, President Macron of France and Chancellor Scholz of Germany." *October 5, 2023*. Accessed April 20, 2024. https://www.consilium.europa.eu/en/press/press-releases/2023/10/05/statement-by-prime-minister-nikol-pashinyan-of-armenia-president-michel-of-the-european-council-president-macron-of-france-and-chancellor-scholz-of-germany/.

Gevorgyan, Valentina. 2023. "The Imperative to Shift Armenia's Peripherality: Contradictions of Institutionalisation and Functioning in Conditions of Democratic Transition." *Journal of Political Science: Bulletin of Yerevan University* 2 (5): 56-75.

Helfrich, Uta. 2023. "Renaissance - ein transnationales neues Narrativ für Europa?" In *Konzepte der NATION im europäischen Kontext im 21. Jahrhundert: Geschichts-, politik- und sprachwissenschaftliche Zugänge*, edited by Aleksandra Salamurović, 87-107. J.B. Metzler, Berlin, Heidelberg.

Kennedy-Pipe, Caroline, and Iftikhar Zaidi. 2021. "The Hybrid Challenge and Small States." In *Small States and the New Security Environment: The World of Small States*, vol 7, edited by Anne-Marie Brady and Baldur Thorhallsson, 27-39. Cham: Springer.

Khvorostiankina, Anna. 2021. "The EU-Armenia Comprehensive and Enhanced Partnership Agreement: A New Instrument of Promoting EU's Values and the General Principles of EU Law." In *EU External Relations Law: Shared Competences and Shared Values in Agreements Between the EU and Its Eastern Neighbourhood*, edited by Stefan Lorenzmeier, Roman Petrov, and Christoph Vedder, 193-226. Cham: Springer.

Klimovich, Stanislav. 2023. "From failed democratization to the war against Ukraine: what happened to Russian institutions under Putin?" *Zeitschrift für Politikwissenschaft* 33: 103-120.

Kocamaz, Sinem Ünaldılar. 2022. "The EU's Promotion of Good Governance and Democracy in the South Caucasus: Regional Strategies and Domestic Constraints." In *EU Good Governance Promotion in the Age of Democratic Decline*, edited by Digdem Soyaltin-Colella, 113-132. Cham: Palgrave Macmillan.

Lavrelashvili, Teona, and Steven Van Hecke. 2023. "The End of Enlargement? The EU's Struggle with the Western Balkans and Eastern Partnership Countries." In *The EU Political System After the 2019 European Elections. Palgrave Studies in European Union Politics*, edited by Olivier Costa, and Steven Van Hecke, 433-454. Palgrave Macmillan.

Lebanidze, Bidzina. 2020. "European and Russian Strategies in the Post-Soviet Space." In *Russia, EU and the Post-Soviet Democratic Failure. Vergleichende Politikwissenschaft*, 125-190. Wiesbaden: Springer VS.

Libaridian, Gerard. 2023. "Why War Won and Negotiations Lost? Is the Absence of War the Same as Peace?" *Journal of Political Science: Bulletin of Yerevan University* 2 (4): 10-26.

Loftus, Suzanne. 2023. Russian-Western Relations: A Trust Never Built. In *Russia, China and the West in the Post-Cold War Era: The Limits of Liberal Universalism*, edited by Suzanne Loftus, 59-91. Palgrave Macmillan, Cham.

Lonardo, Luigi. 2023. Between Law and Geopolitics. In: *EU Common Foreign and Security Policy After Lisbon: Between Law and Geopolitics*, edited by Luigi Lonardo, 133-157. Springer, Cham.

Lucas, Edward, and Bobo Lo. 2022. "Partnership Without Substance: Sino-Russian Relations in Central and Eastern Europe." In *Russia-China Relations: Emerging Alliance or Eternal Rivals?*, edited by Sarah Kirchberger, Svenja Sinjen, and Nils Wörmer, 203-222. Springer, Cham.

Maass, Anna-Sophie. 2019. "The Limits of the European Union's Normative Myth in Armenia and Georgia." In *Democracy Promotion and the Normative Power Europe Framework: The European Union in South Eastern Europe, Eastern Europe, and Central Asia*, edited by Anna-Sophie Maass, 99-117. Cham: Springer

Marsili, Marco. 2021. "The Russian Influence Strategy in Its Contested Neighbourhood." In *The Russian Federation in Global Knowledge Warfare: Influence Operations in Europe and Its Neighbourhood*, edited by Holger Mölder, Vladimir Sazonov, Archil Chochia, and Tanel Kerikmäe, 149-172. Cham: Springer.

MFA of Russia. 2024. "Briefing by the official representative of the Russian Foreign Ministry M.V. Zakharova on current issues of foreign policy." *March 13, 2024.* Accessed April 20, 2024. https://www.youtube.com/watch?v=APqIhte7IK0.

Mission of the RA to the EU. 2024. "Armenia Presents Crossroads of Peace Project at Global Gateway Forum in Brussels." *January 30, 2024.* Accessed April 20, 2024. https://eu.mfa.am/en/news/2024/01/30/armenia-presents-crossroads-of-peace-project-at-global-gateway-forum-in-brussels/12501.

Moore, Gregory J. 2022. "China, Russia and the United States: Balance of Power or National Narcissism?." In: *The United States and Contemporary China-Russia Relations: Theoretical Insights and Implications*, edited by Brandon K. Yoder, 55-77. Palgrave Macmillan, Cham.

Muradov, Ibrahim. 2022. "The Russian hybrid warfare: the cases of Ukraine and Georgia." *Defence Studies* 22 (2): 168-191.

NA of the RA 2024. "Issue regarding ratification of Agreement on status of EU mission in RA debated." *March 19, 2024*. Accessed April 20, 2024. http://www.parliament.am/news.php?cat_id=2&NewsID=20276&year=2024&month=03&day=19&lang=eng.

Ohanyan, Anna. 2021. "Velvet is not a Colour: Armenia's Democratic Transition in a Global Context." In *Armenia's Velvet Revolution: Authoritarian Decline and Civil Resistance in a Multipolar World*, edited by Laurence Broers, and Anna Ohanyan, 25-49. London: I.B. TAURIS.

Oriolo, Anna. 2023. "The Rule of Law, Transnational Crimes, and the Human Rights-Based Approach in the European Union: The Court of Justice as Ultimate Guardian of the 'Good' Laws." In *Solidarity and Rule of Law: The New Dimension of EU Security*, edited by Teresa Russo, Anna Oriolo, and Gaspare Dalia, 201-226. Springer, Cham.

Paturyan, Yevgenya, and Valentina Gevorgyan. 2021. "Civil Society in the Context of Post-Communist Democratisation Discourse." In *Armenian Civil Society. Societies and Political Orders in Transition*, 13-26. Cham: Springer.

Petraitis, Daivis. 2021. "The Russian Doctrine—A Way for the Political Elite to Maximise the Efficiency of Information Warfare." In *The Russian Federation in Global Knowledge Warfare: Influence Operations in Europe and Its Neighbourhood*, edited by Holger Mölder, Vladimir Sazonov, Archil Chochia, and Tanel Kerikmäe, 107-122. Cham: Springer.

Pidkuimukha, Liudmyla. 2023. "Are We Brothers? Pseudo-peaceful Discourse in Russian Media Manipulation." In *Konzepte der NATION im europäischen Kontext im 21. Jahrhundert: Geschichts-, politik- und sprachwissenschaftliche Zugänge*, edited by Aleksandra Salamurović, 159-177. J.B. Metzler, Berlin, Heidelberg.

Politico. 2024. "Armenia moves to expel Russian border guards from Yerevan's airport." *March 7, 2024*. Accessed April 20, 2024. https://www.politico.eu/article/armenia-foreign-minister-ararat-mirzoyan-russia-border-guards-yerevan-zvartnots-airport/.

Politico. 2024. "Russia announces total withdrawal of troops from Nagorno-Karabakh." *April 17, 2024*. Accessed April 20, 2024. https://www.politico.eu/article/russia-withdrawal-troops-nagorno-karabakh-azerbaijan-armenia/.

RFE/RL's Armenian Service. 2024. "Armenia Officially Asks Moscow To Remove Russian Border Troops From Yerevan Airport." *March 06, 2024*. Accessed April 20, 2024. https://www.rferl.org/a/armenia-russian-border-guards-remove-yerevan-airport/32850687.html.

Rouet, Gilles, and Thierry Côme. 2019. "Organisations and Resilience: What Relevance for the Eastern Partnership?" In *Resilience and the EU's Eastern Neighbourhood Countries: From Theoretical Concepts to a Normative Agenda*, edited by Gilles Rouet, and Gabriela Carmen Pascariu, 293-317. Cham: Palgrave Macmillan.

Schatz, Edward. 2023. "Varieties of Authoritarianism in Eurasia." In *Securitization and Democracy in Eurasia: Transformation and Development in the OSCE Region*, edited by Anja Mihr, Paolo Sorbello, and Brigitte Weiffen, 279-290.Cham: Springer.

Simão, Licínia. 2018. "Armenia: Breaking Isolation to Reach Europe." In *The EU's Neighbourhood Policy towards the South Caucasus: Expanding the European Security Community*, edited by Licínia Simão, 147-184. Cham: Palgrave Macmillan.

Slobodnikova, Ivana, Peter Terem, and Radovan Gura. 2019. "Geostrategic Interests of the EU and Their Implementation on the Example of the Ukrainian Crisis." In *Resilience and the EU's Eastern Neighbourhood Countries: From Theoretical Concepts to a Normative Agenda*, edited by Gilles Rouet, and Gabriela Carmen Pascariu, 219-244. Cham: Palgrave Macmillan.

Ter-Matevosyan, Vahram, and Narek Mkrtchyan. 2021. "The Conduct of Armenian Foreign Policy: Limits of the Precarious Balance." In *Small States and the New Security Environment: The World of Small States*, vol 7, edited by Anne-Marie Brady and Baldur Thorhallsson, 203-215. Cham: Springer.

Topychkanov, Petr. 2022. "The Crisis of Nuclear Arms Control amid Russia's Military Offense Against Ukraine." In *Arms Control and Europe: New Challenges and Prospects for Strategic Stability*, edited by Polina Sinovets, and William Alberque, 29-33. Cham: Springer.

Tsybulenko, Evhen, and Aleksi Kajander. 2021. "The Hybrid Arsenal of Russia's War Against the Democratic World." In *The Russian Federation in Global Knowledge Warfare: Influence Operations in Europe and Its Neighbourhood*, edited by Holger Mölder, Vladimir Sazonov, Archil Chochia, and Tanel Kerikmäe, 173-194. Cham: Springer.

Tsygankov, Andrei, Pavel Tsygankov, and Haley Gonzales. 2023. "Putin's "Global Hybrid War": The Anti-Russian Bias of the Atlantic Council." In *Russiagate Revisited: The Aftermath of a Hoax*, edited by Oliver Boyd-Barrett, and Stephen Marmura, 133-159. Palgrave Macmillan, Cham.

Usov, Pavel. 2023. "From Authoritarianism to Neo-Totalitarianism in Belarus." In *Politics and Security of Central and Eastern Europe: Contemporary Challenges*, edited by Ryszard Zięba, 33-56. Cham: Springer.

Vasilyan, Syuzanna. 2020. "'Moral Power' of the EU through its Democracy Promotion Policy in the South Caucasus." In *'Moral Power' of the European Union in the South Caucasus*, edited by Syuzanna Vasilyan, 251-304. London: Palgrave Macmillan.

Wishnick, Elizabeth. 2022. "The Paradox of Sino-Russian Partnership: Global Normative Alignment and Regional Ontological Insecurity." In: *The United States and Contemporary China-Russia Relations: Theoretical Insights and Implications*, edited by Brandon K. Yoder, 155-180. Palgrave Macmillan, Cham.

World Economic Forum. 2024. "Crossroads of Peace: Armenia's call for global cooperation in an evolving world." *January 14, 2024*. Accessed April 20, 2024. https://www.weforum.org/agenda/2024/01/armenia-crossroads-of-peace-global-cooperation/.

Yavuz, M. Hakan, and Michael M. Gunter. 2023. "The Second Nagorno-Karabakh War: Causes and Consequences." In *The Karabakh Conflict Between Armenia and Azerbaijan*, edited by M. Hakan Yavuz, and Michael M. Gunter, 153-193. Cham: Palgrave Macmillan.

Zięba, Ryszard. 2023. "EU and NATO Eastern Policy." In *Politics and Security of Central and Eastern Europe: Contemporary Challenges*, edited by Ryszard Zięba, 119-136. Springer, Cham.

---

[i] EEAS. 2021. "On 1 March 2021, the European Union-Armenia Comprehensive and Enhanced Partnership Agreement (CEPA) will enter into force." Accessed December 20, 2023. https://www.eeas.europa.eu/eeas/eu-and-armenia-comprehensive-and-enhanced-partnership-agreement-enters-force_en.

[ii] The Government of the RA. 2023. ""Crossroads of Peace" project." https://www.gov.am/en/crossroad/; EEAS. 2023. "EU-Armenia: joint press release on the Second Political and Security Dialogue." 15 November 2023, Brussels. https://www.eeas.europa.eu/eeas/eu-armenia-joint-press-release-second-political-and-security-dialogue_en.

[iii] New Azerbaijan Party. 2023. "Official website of the New Azerbaijan Party." November 26, 2023. https://www.yap.org.az; Presidemt.az. 2021. "Opening speech by Ilham Aliyev at the 7th Congress of New Azerbaijan Party." March 5, 2021. https://president.az; Anadolu Ajansı. 2023. "Azerbaijan's president thanks Turkish leader for his speech at UN Ilham Aliyev expresses gratitude to President Recep Tayyip Erdogan for his support for Azerbaijan in his address at 78th UN General Assembly." September 20, 2023. https://www.aa.com.tr/en/europe/azerbaijans-president-thanks-turkish-leader-for-his-speech-at-un/2996399#; Eurasianet. 2023. "Azerbaijan declares victory as surrender talks begin with Karabakh Armenians: Azerbaijan has presented its "reintegration plan" to Karabakhi Armenian representatives. President Aliyev said "all their rights" will be guaranteed." September 21, 2023. https://eurasianet.org/azerbaijan-declares-victory-as-surrender-talks-begin-with-karabakh-armenians.

The EU in Nagorno-Karabakh: Irreversible Rapprochement or Elusive Partnership?

Nino Jibuti

Abstract

For over three decades, the Nagorno-Karabakh enclave has been the place of unresolved ethno-territorial conflict between Armenia and Azerbaijan and a ground for competition between the regional great powers Russia, Türkiye, and Iran as well as the EU. The OSCE Minsk Group was tasked with maintaining security and peace in the region. However, the conflict continued to escalate, leading to the Second Karabakh War in September - November 2020 and eventually to the dissolution of the enclave. Since then, the EU has shown signs of continuing efforts and commitment to being "an honest broker." It intervened and positioned itself as a mediator while the role of Russia was declining amidst the war in Ukraine. Using Critical Discourse Analysis, this chapter will analyze the statements issued by the EU's respective institutions since 2020, in particular the use of language, while addressing the following questions: How and in which regard has the OSCE Minsk Group been ineffective in terms of mediating and reaching sustainable peace since the Second Karabakh war and leading up to the dissolution of the enclave? By scrutinizing the EU-led discourse and its increasingly robust and assertive engagement in the region since the Second Karabakh War, could deploying unarmed civilian observers imply that the EU replaced Russia as a mediator in the conflict? Could the EU's increased interest in seeking alternative energy resources be the reason for its intensified efforts to peacefully settle the conflict?

Keywords: Nagorno-Karabakh conflict; EU; Peace negotiations; OSCE Minsk Group.

Introduction

The South Caucasus along with the Black Sea is one of the strategically important regions in the EaP. The land with ragged mountains and remote valleys has been contested since the 1990s. In September of 2020, a three-decades-long conflict between Armenia and Azerbaijan flared up for the second time. Not only did it claim thousands of people's lives, but it also changed the power architecture in the region. The First and the Second Karabakh wars resulted in major human suffering on both sides. The latter also overturned the 26-year-old status quo, allowing Azerbaijan to reclaim some of the territories. During the first Karabakh War fought around the time of the collapse of the Soviet Union, Yerevan succeeded in capturing Azeri territory that surrounded the largely Armenian-inhabited Nagorno-Karabakh enclave. Even though it was internationally recognized as part of Azerbaijan, the latter was *de facto* united with Armenia.

Russia, the United States, France, the EU, and the member-states of the OSCE endeavored to find a peaceful and sustainable solution to the dispute. In 1995, the United States, France, and Russia assumed the co-chairmanship of the OSCE Minsk Group. They planned to resolve the conflict peacefully by returning some parts of the territory to Azerbaijan while allowing Armenia to obtain a corridor through creating a transitional status for Nagorno-Karabakh.

The following paper, by using content analysis, will discuss the so-called "frozen/unfrozen conflict" metaphor to describe the ethnic conflict between Armenia and Azerbaijan. First, the paper will analyze the weakness that the OSCE Minsk Group demonstrated in developing comprehensive peaceful transformation strategies to find sustainable solutions to the conflict. Second, the paper will attempt to understand the outcomes of the EU's increased engagement in the conflict since the Second Karabakh War (2020). While analyzing the EU's interest in the region as an alternative energy hub, the paper focuses on grasping the language that the EU has used when communicating its stance regarding the war. Thus, the paper aims to provide context, and thought-provoking dilemmas and to fill in the gap in the literature related to the EU's use of language in the conflict by addressing the following questions: How and in which regard has the OSCE Minsk Group been ineffective in terms of mediating in the conflict and reaching a sustainable peace? By scrutinizing the EU's statements and its increasingly robust and assertive engagement in the region since the Second Karabakh War, could deploying unarmed civilian observers imply that the EU replaced Russia as a mediator in the conflict? And could the EU's increased interest in the region to seek alternative energy resources be the reason for its intensified efforts to peacefully settle conflict?

This paper uses a Critical Discourse Analysis (CDA) approach to examine the EU's discourse on the struggle to maintain power in the South Caucasus in the light of the Nagorno-Karabakh war. "Discourse" in this study refers to discourse produced by the people in power who have leverage to influence social and political decisions (van Dijk 1992). That said, CDA focuses on the relationship between language and power. The linguistic approach used in CDA is to view the larger discursive unit of the text as the basic communication unit (Woodak 2009). In that prospect, as Fairclough (2015, 6) writes, CDA is "not just critique of discourse, but also an explanation of how it relates to other elements of the existing reality", again indicating the value of CDA within the field of discourse sociolinguistics. Discourse is a sample of language use, generally written to be spoken, that is, a speech. Theoretically, the concept of power is contested. In a history of theoretical conceptions of power, Hindess (1996) describes three core views of power at the level of the individual. The first view of power is the capacity to act, where people use power over things and people. In this view, there is an unequal relationship between those who use power to alter the political reality. CDA sees language as a social practice and views the context as crucial in its analysis. The linguistic approach used in CDA is to view the larger discursive unit of the text as the basic communication unit. Data analyzed below is collected through the official statements of the EU as well as media outlets since the Second Karabakh War (2020). EU sources include statements issued during 2020-22 by the Council of the European Union, 2013 and 2022, European Council, 2022, European Parliament 2022, and The European Commission 2020 and 2022.

Conceptual Background

After the Bolsheviks conquered Karabakh in the 1920s, Stalin declared that the now-disputed land would be under Azerbaijan's control (De Waal 2005, 17). As a result, when the Nagorno Karabakh Autonomous Republic (NKAO) was formed, 95% of its population was ethnically Armenian, but there was also a significant number of Azeri populations residing in the territory. Now, it is home to roughly 150, 000 people (UNHCR 2022). In the late 1980s, the Soviet Union began to loosen its grip and with the collapse of the Soviet Union, both countries declared independence. In 1988, after passing legislation, Nagorno-Karabakh joined Armenia, even though it was internationally recognized as part of Azerbaijan. Türkiye was the first state to recognize Azerbaijan's independence in 1991, and since then has been a supporter of Azerbaijan and its efforts to consolidate its independence and preserve its territorial integrity, as Ankara realizes its economic potential arising from the rich natural resources of the Caspian Sea.

The conflict between Armenia and Azerbaijan progressed through different stages. In May 1994 a ceasefire was brokered by Russia, but peace remained as elusive as ever. Back in those days, Russia was considered a formal ally of Armenia, but it also had good relations with Azerbaijan. In 2016, the ceasefire agreement was violated, and Armenia and Azerbaijan fought a war that lasted four days (Global Conflict Tracker 2021). In response, the Parliamentary Assembly of the Council of Europe urged the OSCE Minsk Group to support the management of water resources for the inhabitants of the frontier regions of Azerbaijan (Parliamentary Assembly, 2016). The EU called on the OSCE Minsk group to actively participate in managing the situation.

In September 2020, the conflict escalated again, which not only worsened the tension in the region but also involved Russia, the OSCE Minsk Group, and the EU more actively. According to the Madrid Principes, Armenia would cede control of seven Azerbaijani districts that it had occupied but maintain a land corridor to Nagorno-Karabakh and engage in talks on the status of the region. The EU diplomacy offered to facilitate this process by ensuring that both Armenia and Azerbaijan start implementing the Madrid Principles. If both conflicting parties made progress, the EU might have been in a situation to demand once again to contribute to either peacekeeping operations or a post-conflict reconstruction fund or to organize a donors' conference to incentivize Armenia and Azerbaijan to start implementing the principles. In October 2017, the presidents of Armenia and Azerbaijan met in Geneva under the auspices of the Minsk Group, beginning a series of talks on a possible settlement of the conflict. The peace talks progressed until May 2022 with the mediation of the Head of the European Council, Charles Michele, who proposed that Armenia give up part of the land and return it to Azerbaijan. Several thousand opposition supporters rallied in Yerevan to warn the government against concessions on Nagorno-Karabakh. The EU has been very clear in communicating the desire of the heads of the countries to "...move rapidly towards a peace agreement between their countries" (Aljazeera 2022). Fast forward, Baku sent a five-point document to Armenia that suggested the normalization of relations which Armenia accepted. Since the last war, both countries have reportedly expressed their willingness to sign a peace treaty and Azerbaijan pushed those principles while the OSCE Minsk Group and Armenia stressed the need for settlement of the conflict within the framework of the OSCE Minsk Group co-chairmanship to establish regional peace and stability. In light of the Ukrainian war, Russia's focus shifted away from Armenia and the Nagorno-Karabakh. This could have been the opportunity for the EU to interject itself and intensify its efforts to peacefully settle the conflict and for both countries to figure out a way to find common ground.

After Azerbaijan regained control over Nagorno Karabakh in 2023 and formally dissolved the enclave, the EU could engage in facilitating a peace agreement and resolving border issues, connectivity, unblocking transportation links, and working towards long-term sustainable peace.

The EU and the OSCE Minsk Group in the South Caucasus

The EU's bilateral relations with the South Caucasus countries date back to the 1990s. After the collapse of the Soviet Union, the aim was to establish ties, strengthen the newly established states, and cooperate in a multilateral format (Khachatryan 2021).

> "The integration of acceding states increases [the EU's] security but also brings the EU closer to troubled areas... Even in an era of globalization, geography is still important. It is in the European interest that countries on our borders are well-governed..."(Council of the European Union, 2013)

By launching the 2004 European Neighborhood Policy (ENP) and the 2009 Eastern Partnership Policy (EaP), Brussels demonstrated its interest in further enhancing bilateral relations with the South Caucasus countries to build its influence in the region (Khachatryan 2021). The primary purpose of forming the ENP was to strengthen the political and economic capacities and to leverage the EU's power to promote stability in the region (European Commission 2010). There has been a growing expectation among EU member states and partners that the EU take up a more proactive approach when addressing the conflicts in the Eastern neighborhood. Broadly speaking, the EU as a global power could play an important role in reconciliation, reconstruction, and peace consolidation in the region, complementing the OSCE Minsk Group's work and contributing to lasting peace.

The EU has never been directly involved in the Nagorno-Karabakh conflict settlement. It was mainly through the Minsk Group, that it was closely monitoring, observing, and analyzing the situation. After every round of fighting, it provided humanitarian assistance to the conflict-affected population (Wilson 2020). However, it is evident that despite many efforts, 26 years of meetings in the format of the OSCE Minsk Group could not bring about a sustainable solution.

The EU's mediation involvement in the region is important as it is the institution that embodies human rights values and democracy. The EU communicated its involvement in the conflict differently by taking contradictory positions in the ENP Action Plans for Armenia and Azerbaijan, emphasizing territorial integrity on the one hand and the right to self-determination on the other. It should be noted that signing the EU-Armenia Comprehensive and Enhanced Partnership Agreement (CEPA) in 2021 brought the two parties closer together.

"The European Union and its Member States are already providing significant humanitarian assistance to address the immediate needs of the civilian populations affected by the conflict and stand ready to provide further assistance" (Council of the European Union, 19 November 2020).

CEPA provides a framework for the EU and Armenia to work together in a wide range of areas: strengthening democracy, the rule of law and human rights, creating more jobs and business opportunities, improving legislation, public safety, a cleaner environment, as well as better education and opportunities for research. This bilateral agenda also contributes to the EU's overall aim to deepen and strengthen its relations with the countries of its Eastern neighborhood through the Eastern Partnership framework.

"The entry into force of our Comprehensive and Enhanced Partnership Agreement comes at a moment when Armenia faces significant challenges," *said EU High Representative for Foreign Affairs Josep Borrell*. "Across political, economic, trade, and other sectoral areas, our Agreement aims to bring positive change to people's lives, to overcome challenges to Armenia's reforms agenda" (Borrell 2021).

CEPA was signed in November 2017 and substantial parts have been provisionally applied since 1 June 2018. It plays an important role in the modernization of Armenia, through legislative approximation to EU norms in many sectors. This includes reforms in the rule of law and respect for human rights, particularly an independent, efficient, and accountable justice system, as well as reforms aimed at enhancing the responsiveness and effectiveness of public institutions and favoring the conditions for sustainable and inclusive development.

However, before and in the 2020 Nagorno-Karabakh War the EU mostly issued statements of concern, while letting Russia and Türkiye play the key roles and decide the outcomes of the situation.

"Our position is clear: the fighting must stop. Both sides need to re-engage in meaningful negotiations—which, by the way, have not been very fruitful in the last 30 years—without preconditions, under the auspices of the OSCE Minsk Group Co-Chairs. There can be no military solution to the conflict, nor external interference" (European Union, 7 October 2022).

The High Representative of the EU of Foreign Affairs and Security Policy/Vice-President of the European Commission, Josep Borrell, reiterated the need to resume the peace process under the umbrella of the OSCE Minsk Group (Borrell 2020). That said, the EU has a role in resolving this conflict even though it is a long road to freedom and peace.

> "The EU stresses that international humanitarian law must be respected and calls on the parties to implement the agreements on the exchange of prisoners of war and the repatriation of human remains reached within the OSCE Minsk Group Co-Chairs format on 30 October in Geneva" (Council of the European Union, November 19, 2020).

Over the years since establishing the EaP in 2009, this cooperation format has been instrumental in terms of bringing the partner countries closer to the EU. The "20 Deliverables for 2020" have identified the challenges as well as emphasized the key areas such as developing the EaP countries' economy, stronger governance and connectivity, and stronger society to be a priority for the EU. However, the EaP was perceived as a threat to Russia which along with other reasons led to the establishing of the Eurasian Economic Union (EAEU) in 2015 and the pressure on Armenia to become part of this initiative (Delcour and Hoffmann 2018). The consultation report stated that the future cooperation priority areas were set which included integrated economics, accountable institutions, environment and climate resilience, digital transformation, and supporting societies that are more inclusive. Moreover, the report stated that the local conflicts hamper the development of the region. The EU therefore explicitly expressed its interest in security dialogue and practical Common Security and Defense Policy (CSDP) cooperation.

> "... The EU will pursue efforts to support conflict prevention, confidence building, and the facilitation of negotiated peaceful conflict settlements. The EU will also continue assisting populations affected by conflicts to enhance their resilience", (The European Commission in 2020).

In general, the reason that could be considered as the impeding factor in resolving the Nagorno-Karabakh conflict is that it has not been prioritized as one of the pressing issues on the agenda of the EU, NATO, UN, and US. To be precise, the NATO Secretary General has been explicit that the Nagorno-Karabakh conflict is not part of NATO.

"I reminded the [Armenian] president that NATO is not part of this conflict. Both Armenia and Azerbaijan have been valued NATO partners for more than 25 years," said Jens Stoltenberg in a joint news conference with Armenia's President Armen Sarkissian.

It is important to note that the EU faces some power constraints in the region. Another argument that is still debated is that since the EU consists of 27 member states with their foreign policy aspirations and priorities, it puts restraints on the EU to grow its leverage (Gamaghelyan and Rumyantsev 2021). Despite President Macron's outspoken support for peacefully settling the conflict and urging both sides to respect the ceasefire agreement, the EU's influence remained restrained more so until 2020 (Reuters 2020). However, the EU recently revived its position in the region as it lost its grip during the Second Nagorno-Karabakh War. Another issue is Russia, which claims to be making peace in the region and is a co-chair of the OSCE Minsk Group while providing arms to both parties involved in the conflict. Namely, in 2020-21 Armenian imports of major arms from Russia were 94 percent whereas Azerbaijani's 60 percent (SIPRI 2021). As part of Russia's broader military cooperation with Armenia in particular, Russia frequently supplies arms to Armenia at reduced prices, while Azerbaijan pays a full price for the Russian-supplied arms. It can be assumed that economic interests are the primary reason why Russia maintains arms sales deals with Azerbaijan (ibid).

On 30 September 2020, the President of the European Council Charles Michel expressed his deep concern over the escalated conflict and called on both State presidents for an immediate cease-fire. He stated that the only way out of this situation was to settle the conflict and expressed his interest in supporting the OSCE in the mediation process (Charles Michel, Twitter 2020). A year later, in November 2021, he assessed releasing detainees and maps of mined areas positively and reiterated that the EU supports, and will continue to support this process (Charles Michel, Twitter 2021). This gesture could underpin that the EU and the European Council specifically have an interest in supporting the OSCE Minsk Group to work on finding more sustainable solutions.

Certainly, the US and the EU remain important actors in the region, but it can be assumed that their role is declining. Azerbaijan and the West's interests have drifted away with human rights issues intervening and Baku accusing the OSCE Minsk Group of failing in the negotiation process (Kalfayan 2020). Moreover, neither the US nor France have made any tangible contributions to solving the conflict which caused Azerbaijan's distrust of the establishment and considered it to be biased. For Baku, a large Armenian population residing in France and the US was the reason for distrust, and considered the US and France as dishonest negotiators with biased stances (Stronski 2021).

Currently, the West is occupied with its own domestic political and social issues and the war in Ukraine. The latter certainly bogged down Russia and limited its interference in the conflict. Even though the OSCE Minsk Group lost its credibility as well as legitimacy and had a very limited role in the peace talks process, enhancing this format could be an interesting approach, especially for Armenia as its bargaining positions are weakened (Meister 2021). The Armenian Prime Minister Nikol Pashinyan took a critical stance and called for an OSCE fact-finding mission to be deployed to the Lachin corridor; he also appealed to the International Court of Justice (ICJ). For more than four months Nagorno-Karabakh had been under a blockade, lacking vital supplies and causing a humanitarian emergency (Kinninmont 2023).

The U.S. has an important role to play apart from being one of the co-chairs of the OSCE Minsk Group. Given the continued instability and bloodshed in the region, it is crucially important that the EU and the US step up and continue their efforts to find a diplomatic solution to this conflict. It could be assumed that Brussel's focus is not exactly the South Caucasus but issues in the region could cause problems for the EU in the future which are related to transportation, energy resources, etc. In addition, since the 2020 war, Azerbaijan cultivated closer ties with Russia which further complicates the process, and Russia embraces those connections with Azerbaijan.

If the EU aspires to gain some amount of dominance and restore its image in the eyes of the conflicting partners, it could interject and provide funding for reconstruction through the European Investment Bank (EIB). The EU has held a series of discussions, bringing the conflicting parties to one table, including a trilateral meeting in May 2022 which was assessed as "frank and productive" (Michel 2022). Since the launch of the full-scale war in Ukraine, the EU intensified its efforts to serve as a mediator between the conflicting countries. Connectivity, peace agreement, and socio-economic development issues were discussed during the meeting. It could be said that the discussion orchestrated by the EU was a step forward in the process and the EU's involvement in the process is notable (European Parliament 2022). Earlier, the EU issued statements of concern about the blockage of the Lachin Corridor between the decades-long foes.

> "The EU will take forward with both parties the work of the Economic Advisory Group, which seeks to advance economic development for the benefit of both countries and their populations" (European Council, May 23, 2022).

In addition, technical expertise as well as border management programs could provide the impetus for long-awaited peace and stability in the region as well as unlocking regional connectivity (Dreyfus and Hugot 2021). This kind of EU support could restore, to some extent, the deteriorated relationships between Brussels, Baku, and Yerevan. In 2022, the EU Civil Mission to observe the border with Azerbaijan was deployed under a two-month mandate. Given that Azerbaijan and the EU signed a new memorandum on diversification of fossil-fuel energy sources, readiness to deliver gas through the Southern Gas Corridor underlines the importance of the EU's interest in maintaining peace and stability in the region. In 2022, the EU called on Azerbaijan to ensure freedom and security of movement along the Lachin Corridor and suggested dialogue and consultations with the parties involved (EEAS Press, 13 December 2022). The principal judicial organ of the UN ordered provisional measures that Azerbaijan end the blockage of the Lachin Corridor (ICJ 2023). However, it did not translate to a tangible action.

The EU deploying an unarmed civilian mission in Armenia has been ground-breaking and speaks about the EU's growing interest in the region. That way Brussels could be informed about the flareups immediately, providing an opportunity to intervene promptly to maintain peace and guard the borders. The gesture that Armenia made, to invite EU observers shows that it is no longer willing to rely on its decades-long strategic partner, Russia.

The question to be asked is if there are any prospects of ending the conflict with tangible results that bring peace and security to the region when there are powerful actors such as Russia and Türkiye that shape the agenda for peace resolution. The current situation is certainly looking more hopeful in terms of finding common ground between the conflicting countries. This bold move was called "a new phase of EU engagement in the South Caucasus" by Joseph Borrell (Carnegie, 2023).

The EU has vast experience in promoting dialogue and resolving conflict with peaceful means. The European Parliament expressed its commitment to continue to support this process using soft instruments. The EU could support CSOs from both countries to organize joint initiatives and engage with Armenians in Karabakh which is crucial for reaching sustainable peace (European Parliament 2022). Thus, the EU could potentially become a more reliable partner for Armenia and an opportunity for the EU to sideline Moscow (Carnegie 2023).

While a complicated situation between Armenia and Azerbaijan persists in the region, the EU's increased involvement could still be assessed positively, considering that the EU has been more outspoken about the conflict, taking action on the ground to monitor the border, and urging for the opening of the Lachin Corridor.

The EU's Growing Interest in the South Caucasus as an Energy Hub

The outbreak of the Second Karabakh War in 2020 and the full-scale war in Ukraine in 2022 have vastly questioned the security environment in the region: Türkiye strengthened its dominance and brought Iran into the picture, which put the countries in a vulnerable position in terms of security. Türkiye is expanding its military presence in the South Caucasus, the Balkans, and the Middle East by employing coercive diplomacy to resolve foreign policy issues (Mehmetcik and Çelik 2022). Azerbaijan, which is backed by Israel and Türkiye, is more confident about winning this battle than ever. The regional platforms are important for the EU's peacekeeping and conflict resolution efforts. It would be fair to assume that the Karabakh conflict has had a significant impact on the political, economic, and most of all security issues in the region. For instance, the 3+3 Regional Cooperation initiative was an attempt to change the balance of power and increase Russia's dominance in the region. After the Second Nagorno-Karabakh War in 2021, the Turkish President suggested creating a Six Country Regional Cooperation platform that included the three states from the South Caucasus (Armenia, Azerbaijan, and Georgia) and three great powers: Türkiye, Russia, and Iran. On 6 October 2021, Russian Foreign Minister Sergey Lavrov announced Moscow was committed to the establishment of a new 3+3 format to "address the issues of security and unblocking economic and transport ties (Teslova 2021). However, this initiative was not fully endorsed by Georgia, as it would be yet another tool for Russia to undermine Georgia's territorial integrity and expand Russia's power advantage in the region. Additionally, the 3+3 format would not provide any additional incentive for Georgia, as it has been part of the largest infrastructural projects in the region, namely the Tbilisi-Baku-Ceyhan and Southern Gas Corridor projects. Georgia has shown its commitment to working with its neighbors; however, partnership with Russia in any format is not an option. Apart from that, the absence of a counterbalance of the Western countries in the cooperation could potentially question the security of the region and give dominance to the great powers in the region. That said, considering the actors involved in the 3+3 cooperation initiative, Georgia would align with its long-time foe Russia and to some extent question its Western orientation (Samkharadze 2021). Georgia has proved itself to have the capability to mediate the conflict. This was proven by the recent US- and Georgia-brokered deal, which released 15 Armenian detainees for which Yerevan in exchange provided the map of landmines of the Agdam district. It took place in neutral territory—the Georgia-Azerbaijan border. European as well as American actors along with Georgia facilitated this process. This action was claimed to be a step forward for "…bettering the security architecture of the South Caucasus' (Civil.ge 2021). In this process, Georgia can be seen as a support to fostering a more neutral and result-oriented platform by participating in the infrastructural and economic initiatives.

While other foreign actors have somewhat defined stances in the conflict, Russia plays contradictory roles in this war game: it has the power to shape the political processes and does everything in its power to retain its position and remain an influential player. During the outbreaks of a series of conflicts, Russia has been providing arms to both countries, and it serves Russia well to ensure tension between Armenia and Azerbaijan (Aljazeera 2021). Moreover, since signing the Collective Security Treaty Organization (CSTO) in 1997, for the first time Armenia called on Russia to provide a security assistance response which could indicate that Russia's influence is only getting stronger in the region. "Given the current situation, I think it makes sense to consider the question of stationing outposts of Russian border guards along the entire length of the Armenian-Azeri border", Pashinyan (2021) declared. However, when the CSTO declined to respond to Armenia's call for help, this served as an opportunity for the EU to further engage in peacefully settling the conflict.

In light of the ongoing energy crisis in Europe, the EU has been working intensively with international partners to diversify supplies and mitigate the rise in energy prices. Azerbaijan in particular could become an important energy provider for the EU. Therefore, the EU is not interested in creating tensions and jeopardizing its relationship with Azerbaijan. The Commission went so far as to acknowledge the role of the Southern Gas Corridor (SGC) which could help the EU to secure reliable natural gas supplies.

> "Azerbaijan has already increased the natural gas deliveries to the EU and this trend will continue, with up to 4 billion cubic meters of additional gas this year and volumes expected to more than double by 2027" (European Commission, 18 July 2022).

The South Caucasus Region is geopolitically and economically important, as it connects Asia and Europe and creates prospects for the development of the region and cooperation opportunities with different foreign countries. As an example, in February 2021 the first direct train reached Tbilisi from China, demonstrating the potential of connecting Asia and Europe by offering high-speed sea-rail connections through the Black Sea, Mediterranean, and beyond (IPN Interpress News 2021). Türkiye considers Azerbaijan a strategic partner for its gas and oil resources and is getting closer to connecting the resources of the Caspian Sea to Europe. Even though Azerbaijan competes with Russia in natural gas and oil, it balances this by purchasing weapons from Russia with the money it earns. The Commission recognized that the SGC plays a key role in the diversification of natural gas supply to the EU, for Southeastern European countries (European Commission, 18 July 2022). Additionally, as part of the economic and investment plan of the EaP, the EU is willing to invest 2.3 billion in Georgia-Romania Black Sea submarine electricity cable for increased mutual resilience, creating transport projects and reinforcing trade routes to the EU, along with digital connectivity projects (European Commission, 17 December 2022). This could be a way for the EU to gain a presence in the region and an opportunity for countries such as Georgia, Armenia, and Azerbaijan to create closer ties with the EU.

When it comes to energy resource diversification, the EU has played a crucial role in ensuring the availability of affordable supplies of energy since 2020. The SGC is an important infrastructural project that connects the Caspian Sea basin with the EU. The Memorandum of Understanding on a Strategic Partnership in the Field of Energy only strengthens the existing cooperation between the EU and Azerbaijan.

> "Today, with this new Memorandum of Understanding, we are opening a new chapter in our energy cooperation with Azerbaijan, a key partner in our efforts to move away from Russian fossil fuels. Not only are we looking to strengthen our existing partnership which guarantees stable and reliable gas supplies to the EU via the Southern Gas Corridor. We are also laying the foundations of a long-term partnership on energy efficiency and clean energy, as we both pursue the objectives of the Paris Agreement. But energy is only one of the areas where we can enhance our cooperation with Azerbaijan and I look forward to tapping the full potential of our relationship" (European Commission,18 July 2022).

Several actions have been carried out from the EU's end to support the further expansion of the SGC. Within the framework of the REPowerEU plan, the EU energy sector has strengthened its ties with Azerbaijan. The EU has been very proactive in terms of enhancing the internal EU network to accommodate the increased need for energy in Europe and to reduce dependence on a single resource. It should be noted that the current infrastructure requires development, modernization, and enhancement, which could enable the gas flow from SGC to Bulgaria (European Commission 2022).

> "Commissioned at the end of 2020, the Southern Gas Corridor delivered 8.1 billion cubic meters (bcm) of gas to Europe in 2021, and 11.4 bcm in 2022,

representing respectively 2.4% and 3.4% of total EU gas imports. It is expected that gas deliveries via the Southern Gas Corridor will remain at the level of 12 bcm of gas in 2023" (European Commission 2022).

The opening of the transportation links in the region was also part of the Russia-brokered ceasefire agreement; however, the situation remains tense. Despite the complicated geopolitical constellation in the region, reopening the Araxes Rail Link could potentially provide Armenia, Azerbaijan, Türkiye, Iran, and Russia with a more cost-effective transportation route for supplies and goods, on the other hand, it could support the development of Nakhichevan. This historical cooperation could unblock the transportation corridors and an alternative transportation route an opportunity for East Asia, Azerbaijan, and Armenia to create more ecologically sustainable and cost-effective transportation and trade routes. If this issue is settled, this could mean that neighbors would resume trade relations and could provide the impetus for normalizing political relations. That said, it could also serve as an opportunity to reduce tension between the conflicting parties (Dreyfus and Hugot 2021). Later, however, Armenian Foreign Minister Ararat Mirzoyan stated in Paris on 11 November 2021 that there was a new wave of pre-conditions set by Türkiye that could delay this process (Radio Free Europe 2021). For Georgia, this would mean losing an East-West transit route role (Meister 2021). It is a historical event and yet we shall see if it produces any positive results in terms of settling the conflict between the two countries.

Russia's war in Ukraine has taken its attention away from the Nagorno-Karabakh conflict. As Moscow is preoccupied with the war in Ukraine and confrontational rhetoric with the West, its Western neighboring countries are reassessing their security issues. This could be a window of opportunity for the parties involved in the conflict to use the EU's leverage to find solutions and settle the conflict with the EU's mediation. Considering the potential that the EU seeks in terms of diversification of energy sources for Europe, this could put the region in an advantaged position—maintaining peace and stability in the region is one of the key priorities.

Conclusion

After the recent war between Azerbaijan and Armenia over Nagorno-Karabakh, the EU intensified its effort to de-escalate regional tension and peacefully resolve the conflict between the decade-long post-Soviet foes. About 15 years ago, the EU was willing to mediate the dispute between the two countries; however, peace seemed to be elusive at that time. Placing a civilian mission could be understood as an attempt to take action, sideline the Russian peacekeeping mission, and lower the risk of further complications. The EU tried to play a more significant role in the Nagorno-Karabakh conflict but quickly became bogged down in multiple disagreements within the bloc and between Azerbaijan and Armenia.

Since the Second Karabakh War, the EU has changed its language and approach. Analyzing the statements issued by the EU, it is noticeable that while its support was originally focused on humanitarian assistance, confidence building, expressing deep concerns, and assisting conflict-affected populations on the ground, since 2022 the EU has become more adamant and proactive, urging both countries to address the conflict through peaceful means.

Interest in utilizing energy resources brought the EU's attention to Nagorno-Karabakh and more so to Azerbaijan. The EU has always avoided becoming directly involved in the conflict as it did not want to compete with Russia for influence in the region. However, it would be fair to assume that the recent economic relation-building with Azerbaijan, e.g. through enhancing cooperation in the energy and transport sectors, has increased the EU's presence in the region. The EU has been working intensively to diversify energy supplies. This increased cooperation and working together for their combined interest gives Azerbaijan an authority and advantage in the region to dictate its interests and desires when it comes to reclaiming the Nagorno-Karabakh enclave. The EU-backed economic cooperation and dependence thus create a conducive environment for Azerbaijan to influence the current conflict by tilting outcomes in its favor and regaining the Nagorno-Karabakh territories.

The OSCE Minsk Group as well as the EU's efforts in conflict mediation were missing the systematic approach to pressure both conflicting countries to reach solutions. While NATO opted not to get involved in the conflict, the EU supported conflict resolution mostly by issuing formal statements of concern. Those concerns did not translate into tangible solutions and were mostly worrying messages. What we are now seeing is that more than ever the EU is stepping up its efforts to support the conflict-affected population in and around Nagorno-Karabakh and to monitor Armenia's volatile border with Azerbaijan, bolstering its role in the region.

The EU's involvement could be called a neutrality game for several reasons. First, until now neither Armenia nor Azerbaijan saw the EU as a medium to help them settle the conflict peacefully. Neither country asked the EU to support them in this process. Armenia was careful about involving the EU in the process as it could potentially irritate Russia. On the other hand, Azerbaijan was worried about its demonstrated neutrality. It was becoming more skeptical about the international community's efforts to resolve the conflict. The EU's effort to develop an outreach plan for the South Caucasus through the ENP did not mention much about the conflict while it outlined several different areas and sectors for cooperation. It could be assumed that appointing the Special Representative for the South Caucasus and Crisis in Georgia back in 2003 was a message from the EU that it was ready to show more commitment and was restlessly searching for ways to settle the conflict. But while it could do so for the crisis in Georgia (Abkhazia and South Ossetia), it was not possible to do the same for Nagorno-Karabakh as Azerbaijan showed reluctance in this process.

The EU's recent attempt to find ways to settle the Nagorno-Karabakh conflict could open the door to re-energize diplomacy by implementing the Madrid Principles. However, the EU can only provide such help with the consent of Armenia, Azerbaijan, and the OSCE Minsk Group co-chairs. The conditions for the EU to have a substantial impact on the conflict are not much better than they were a decade and a half ago. However, the difference now is that the EU now sees a potential partner in Azerbaijan due to a common interest in the energy and transportation sectors.

Considering the EU's interests in the region and siding with Azerbaijan could mean that it is becoming a stronger and more influential player. It could complement the OSCE Minsk Group's effort to mediate the conflict while acknowledging the other regional player's interests. Russia's war in Ukraine could be a window of opportunity for the EU to demonstrate its efforts to mediate the conflict.

Bibliography

Al Jazeera. 2020. "The EU Suffered a Major Loss in Nagorno-Karabakh." https://www.aljazeera.com/opinions/2020/11/23/the-biggest-loser-in-nagorno-karabkh-is-not-armenia.

Al Jazeera. 2020. "What's Türkiye's Role in the Nagorno-Karabakh Conflict?" https://www.aljazeera.com/features/2020/10/30/whats-Türkiyes-role-in-the-nagorno-karabakh-conflict.

Al Jazeera. 2021. "Armenia Seeks Russian Forces on Azerbaijan Border amid Tensions." https://www.aljazeera.com/news/2021/7/29/armenia-seeks-russian-forces-on-azerbaijan-border-amid-tensions.

Al Jazeera. 2022. "Armenia, Azerbaijan Gear up for Nagorno-Karabakh Peace Talks." https://www.aljazeera.com/news/2022/4/7/armenia-azerbaijan-gear-up-for-nagorno-karabakh-peace-talks.

Anadolou Ajansi. 2021. "NATO is not part of the conflict in Nagorno-Karabakh." https://www.aa.com.tr/en/azerbaijan-front-line/nato-is-not-part-of-conflict-in-nagorno-karabakh/2014457.

BBC News. 2020. "Armenia, Azerbaijan and Russia Sign Nagorno-Karabakh Peace Deal." https://www.bbc.com/news/world-europe-54882564.

Azatutyun Radio. 2021. "De Waal: Russia Is Playing a Long Game in Armenian-Azerbaijani Conflict" https://www.azatutyun.am/a/31423368.html.

Civil.ge. 2021. "Georgia-US Mediation: Azerbaijan Swaps 15 Armenian Captivities for Mine Maps" https://civil.ge/archives/427221.

Council on Foreign Relations. 2021. "Nagorno-Karabakh Conflict." https://www.cfr.org/global-conflict-tracker/conflict/nagorno-karabakh-conflict.

Council of the European Union. 2014. *A Secure Europe in a Better World.* European Security Strategy. Brussels, 2013.

Carnegie. 2023. Could the New EU Mission Sideline Russia in Armenia-Azerbaijan Settlement?" https://carnegieendowment.org/politika/89060.

Council of the European Union. 19 November 2020. "Nagorno-Karabakh: Declaration by the High Representative on behalf of the European Union". https://www.consilium.europa.eu/en/press/press-releases/2020/11/19/nagorno-karabakh-declaration-by-the-high-representative-on-behalf-of-the-european-union/.

Council of the European Union, 19 November 2020. "Nagorno-Karabakh: Declaration by the High Representative on behalf of the European Union". https://www.consilium.europa.eu/en/press/press-releases/2020/11/19/nagorno-karabakh-declaration-by-the-high-representative-on-behalf-of-the-european-union/.

Delcour Laure and Katharina Hoffmann. 2018. "The EU's Policy in the South Caucasus", *L'Europe en Formation*, 385: 7-25. https://www.cairn.info/revue-l-europe-en-formation-2018-1-page-7.htm.

De Waal, Thomas. 2005. "The Nagorny Karabakh Conflict: Origins, Dynamics, and Misconceptions", in Laurence Broers (ed.). *The Limits of Leadership Elites and Societies in the Nagorny Karabakh Peace Process*, Conciliation Resources London, 12-17. https://www.c-r.org/accord/nagorny-karabakh/nagorny-karabakh-conflict-origins-dynamics-and-misperceptions.

De Waal, Thomas. 2021. "Unfinished Business in the Armenia-Azerbaijan Conflict." Carnegie Europe. https://carnegieeurope.eu/2021/02/11/unfinished-business-in-armenia-azerbaijan-conflict-pub-83844.

Dreyfus, Emanuel and Jules Hugot. 2021. "Opening the Araxes Rail Link between Armenia and Azerbaijan: Why the EU Should Support the Connection". *Ponars Eurasia*. https://www.ponarseurasia.org/opening-the-araxes-rail-link-between-armenia-and-azerbaijan-why-the-eu-should-support-the-connection/?fbclid=IwAR1lHdIExFx_LK7oCnSdiS4PuzxPJvKXU2rYe5Y5-dHvWTXu89YkieJx0B0.

Eurasianet. 2021. "The EU and Karabakh: Picking up the Pieces, Looking for a Role." https://eurasianet.org/perspectives-the-eu-and-karabakh-picking-up-the-pieces-looking-for-a-role.

Eurasianet. 2021. "Heavy Fighting Breaks out between Armenia and Azerbaijan." https://eurasianet.org/heavy-fighting-breaks-out-between-armenia-and-azerbaijan?fbclid=IwAR3ocy70NmBSFSxU-Jax17HqwazJQVw5v-UMPPkY1OVQ8DhJvxdJ1X7X9SA.

European Commission. 2020. "Eastern Partnership Policy beyond 2020", Brussels, SWD (2020) 56 final https://eeas.europa.eu/sites/default/files/1_en_act_part1_v6.pdf.

Financial Times. 2020. "Armenia Calls for Russian Help as Fight with Azerbaijan Intensifies", https://www.ft.com/content/9ca3163a-d267-4ac2-bfc3-77f86995dc75.

European Commission. 2022. "EU and Azerbaijan Enhance Bilateral Relations, Including Energy Cooperation." https://ec.europa.eu/commission/presscorner/detail/en/IP_22_4550.

European Commission. 2022. "Statement by President von der Leyen at the Signing Ceremony of the Memorandum of Understanding for the Development of the Black Sea Energy Submarine Cable" https://ec.europa. eu/commission/presscorner/detail/en/statement_22_7807.

European Commission. 2022. "Diversification of Gas Supply Sources and Routes." https://energy.ec.europa.eu/topics/energy-security/diversifi cation-gas-supply-sources-and-routes_en.

European Commission. 2020. "20 Deliverables for 2020." https://www.cons ilium.europa.eu/en/policies/eastern-partnership/20-deliverables-for-2020/.

European Commission. 2022. "EU and Azerbaijan Enhance Bilateral Relations, Including Energy Cooperation." https://ec.europa.eu/commission/pre sscorner/detail/en/IP_22_4550.

European Union External Action. 2022. "Armenia/Azerbaijan: Statement by the Spokesperson on the Developments around the Lachin Corridor." https://www.eeas.europa.eu/eeas/armeniaazerbaijan-statement-spo kesperson-developments-around-lachin-corridor_en.

European Council, 23 May 2022. "Press Statement by President Michel of the European Council Following a Trilateral Meeting with President Aliyev of Azerbaijan and Prime Minister Pashinyan of Armenia". https://www. consilium.europa.eu/en/press/press-releases/2022/05/23/press-sta tement-by-president-michel-of-the-european-council-following-a-trila teral-meeting-with-president-aliyev-of-azerbaijan-and-prime-minister -pashinyan-of-armenia/.

European Union External Action. 7 October 2022. "Nagorno Karabakh: Remarks by the High Representative / Vice-President Josep Borrell at the EP Plenary Debate on the Resumption of Hostilities between Armenia and Azerbaijan". https://www.eeas.europa.eu/eeas/nagorno-karabak h-remarks-high-representative-vice-president-josep-borrell-ep-plena ry-debate_en.

European Commission, The European Neighbourhood Policy, quoted in Laure Delcour, "The European Union, A Security Provider in the Eastern Neighbourhood?" *European Security* 19(4): 535–549.

European Parliament. The European Union's Relations with Armenia and Azerbaijan. 2022. www.europarl.europa.eu/RegData/etudes/STUD/20 22/734676/EPRS_STU(2022)734676_EN.pdf.

Gamaghelyan, Philip and Sergey Rumyantsev. 2021. "The Road to the Second Karabakh War: The Role of Ethno-centric Narratives in the Nagorno-Karabakh Conflict". *Caucasus Survey*, 9(3): 320-336.

Gonca, Isa Burak. 2016. "Nagorno-Karabakh: Armenia's Claims, Azerbaijan's Position, and the Peace Efforts", *E-International Relations*, https://www.e-ir.info/2016/06/04/nagorno-karabakh-armenias-claims-azerbaijans-position-and-the-peace-efforts/.

Hindess, Barry. 1996. *Discourses of Power. From Hobbes to Foucault*. Oxford.

International Court of Justice. 2023. Press Release, No. 2023/10. https://www.icj-cij.org/sites/default/files/case-related/180/180-20230222-PRE-01-00-EN.pdf.

International Institute for Peace. 2021. "Western Balkans Initiative." https://www.iipvienna.com/western-balkan-initiative.

IPN Interpress News. 2021. "The First Blockchain to Arrive from China in Georgia." https://www.interpressnews.ge/en/article/111881-first-direct-blocktrain-to-arrive-from-china-in-georgia

Irish, John. 2021. "Frances's Maron proposes New Talks on the Nagorno-Karabakh", *Reuters*, https://www.reuters.com/article/us-armenia-azerbaijan-france-idUSKBN26N36K.

Kalfayan, Philippe. 2020. "A Closer Look at the Trilateral Agreement to End War." https://mirrorspectator.com/2020/11/16/a-closer-look-at-the-trilateral-agreement-to-end-war/.

Khachatryan, Hamsik. 2021. "Geopolitical Reshuffling in the South Caucasus in the Aftermath of the 2020 Nagorno-Karabakh War and the EU's Policy Options", Georgian Institute of Politics Policy Brief, issue #35, https://www.scribd.com/document/538834319/Policy-Brief-35#download&from_embedb.

Mehmetcik, Hakan and Arda Can Çelik. 2022. "The Militarization of Türkiye's Foreign Policy". *Journal of Balkan and Near Eastern Studies* 24(1): 24-41.

Meister, Stefan., "Shifting Geopolitical Realities in the South Caucasus", Utrikapolitika Institutet, SCEEUS Reports on Human Rights and Security in Eastern Europe No. 8, https://www.ui.se/forskning/centrum-for-ost europastudier/sceeus-report/shifting-geopolitical-realities-in-the-south-caucasus/?fbclid=IwAR13sxOPO38EAmVAlTMtvFUwuV47NMKfuJE yFD03JX4xh5fIoto-48SD3vE.

Michel, Charles. 2020. Tweet, https://twitter.com/eucopresident/status/1311331261772967936.

Michel, Charles. 2021. Tweet, https://twitter.com/eucopresident/status/1403740999407517697.

Minority Rights Group International, 2018. World Directory of Minorities and Indigenous Peoples—Nagorny Karabakh (unrecognized state), April, https://www.refworld.org/docid/4954ce4b23.html.

Novikova, Gayane. 2017. "Armenia: Some Features of Internal (in)stability", *Caucasus Survey*, 5(2): 177-194.

Ohanyan, Anna. 2020. "Russia and the West Still Need Each Other in Nagorno-Karabakh." https://carnegieendowment.org/2020/11/24/russia-and-west-still-need-each-other-in-nagorno-karabakh-pub-83295.

Parliamentary Assembly of the Council of Europe. 2016. Inhabitants of Frontier Regions of Azerbaijan are Deliberately Deprived of Water, Resolution 2085 (2016). https://pace.coe.int/en/files/22429/html.

President of Russia. 2020. Statement by President of the Republic of Azerbaijan, Prime Minister of the Republic of Armenia and President of the Russian Federation. http://en.kremlin.ru/events/president/news/64384.

Radio Free Europe/Radio Liberty. 2020. "Five Key Things to Know About Nagorno-Karabakh." https://www.rferl.org/a/30893222.html.

Radio Free Europe/Radio Liberty. 2021. "Armenia Accuses Türkiye of Setting 'New Conditions' for Improving Ties." https://www.rferl.org/a/armenia-azerbaijan-Türkiye-nakhichevan-corridor/31571713.html?fbclid=IwAR00qzzZC7OK9QbHTEHJ78z-F5cec5boQTfA-caYpQ3PtL3dUiotT0gyRgs.

Samkharadze, Nino. 2021. "Georgia's 3+3 Dilemma: Regional Leadership or Falling into the Aggressor Neighbor's Trap?" http://gip.ge/georgias-33-dilemma-regional-leadership-or-falling-into-the-aggressor-neighbors-trap/.

Stockholm International Peace Research Institute. 2021. "Arms Transfers to Conflict Zones: The Case of Nagorno-Karabakh" https://www.sipri.org/commentary/topical-backgrounder/2021/arms-transfers-conflict-zones-case-nagorno-karabakh.

Stronski, Paul. 2021. "The Shifting Geography of the South Caucasus", Carnegie Endowment for International Peace. https://carnegieendowment.org/2021/06/23/shifting-geography-of-south-caucasus-pub-84814.

Teslova, Elena. "Russia Suggests 3+3 Format with Türkiye, Iran, Azerbaijan, Armenia, Georgia in the Caucasus." https://www.aa.com.tr/en/politics/russia-suggests-3-3-format-with-Türkiye-iran-azerbaijan-armenia-georgia-in-caucasus/2384679.

The Prime Minister of the Republic of Armenia. 2020. Statement by the Prime Minister of The Republic of Armenia, the President of the Republic of Azerbaijan, and the President of the Russian Federation. https://www.primeminister.am/en/press-release/item/2020/11/10/Announcement/.

UNHCR. 2020. Armenia. https://www.unhcr.org/countries/armenia.

UNICEF. 2020. Statement of One Month Fighting in and beyond Nagorno-Karabakh. https://www.unicef.org/press-releases/unicef-statement-one-month-fighting-and-beyond-nagorno-karabakh.

Van Dijk, Teun. 1992. "Discourse and the Denial of Racism". *Discourse and Society* 3: 87-118.

Wilson, James., 2020, "EU Aid for Nagorno-Karabakh", EU Political Report. https://www.eupoliticalreport.eu/eu-aid-for-nagorno-karabakh/.

Wodak, Ruth and Michael Meyer. 2009. *Methods of Critical Discourse Analysis*, Thousand Oaks CA.

Bios

Ashot Aleksanyan is a Doctor of Sciences (Political Sciences), Professor and Head of the Chair of Political Science of Faculty of International Relations, as well as Lecturer at the Center for European Studies of Yerevan State University. He is editor-in-chief of the Journal of Political Science: Bulletin of Yerevan University. His main interests are civil society, European integration, human political rights and freedoms. He has been a DAAD-Visiting Scientist at the Institute of Political Science of Leibniz University of Hannover (2002-2009), DAAD-Visiting Scientist at the Geschwister Scholl Institute of Political Science of Ludwig-Maximilian University of Munich (2013) and the Institute for East European Studies of Free University of Berlin (2016), as well as the EU Erasmus Mundus «ALRAKIS» project Visiting Scientist at the Faculty of Social Sciences of the Katholieke Universiteit Leuven (2012). Since 2016, he has been an international fellow of the Institute of Political Science at the Friedrich-Schiller-University Jena.

Anahit Babayan is a young researcher. She has held positions as the Assistant of UNESCO Chair on Human Rights, Democracy and Political Science at Brusov State University, indicating her involvement in academic and research activities related to these fields. As a lecturer, her primary subject being Political Science suggests her deep understanding and interest in political dynamics, both domestically and internationally. Her research interests include but are not limited to the Caucasus region, foreign policy and integration processes of post-Soviet states, conflicts, Europeanization, and democratization. She earned her Master's degree in European Studies from Brusov State University in Armenia.

Giorgi Beridze is an invited lecturer at the Department of Political Science at Tbilisi State University. He is currently working on a PhD thesis on labour policy-making and business elites, which will describe the changes in policymaking in Georgia following the signing of the Association Agreement with the EU in 2014. His works also include history of Marxist movement in Georgia, labor history, labor rights and the theory of Europeanization. The author has recently been appointed as Head of Department for the Study of Archives of the Democratic Republic and Recent History of Georgia at the Ivane Javakhishvili Tbilisi State University Library where his research is about history of the Social Democracy in Georgia during and after the Russian Revolution. His articles have been published in various peer-reviewed journals, including *Europe-Asia Studies* and *Eastern European Regional Studies*.

Gvantsa Davitashvili is a Professor at New Vision University, where she teaches Europeanisation and European Integration courses. She has experience teaching at HEI on national and international levels for more than 10 years. Prof. Davitashvili has experience working for the protection, promotion and research of human rights at NHRIs (Public Defender Office of Georgia, Transparency International Georgia, American Bar Association/Rule of Law Initiative) for more than 10 years. She is an affiliated policy analyst at the Georgian Institute of Politics. Prof. Davitashvili holds a Ph.D. degree in International Relations at the University of Basque Country and an LL.M in South-East European Law and European Integration at the University of Graz. Her research interests include European integration of the Eastern Partnership countries, external Europeanisation, democratization, and EU foreign policy. She is the author of several publications, as well as commentaries and study resources.

Ruben Elamiryan is an Associate Professor at the Department of World Politics and International Relations at Russian-Armenian University. He is also an Associate Professor at the Public Administration Academy of the Republic of Armenia. He received his PhD in Political Science (International Relations) in 2014 from the Academic Council at the National Strategic Research Institute under the Ministry of Defense of Armenia. His thesis is entitled, 'The problem of Information security in the context of providing the National Interest of the Republic of Armenia'. He has more than ten years' experience in academic research and lecturing, starting from 2010, when he began his PhD studies. From September 2018 to August 2019 he undertook a Visiting Fulbright Scholar position at Princeton University, working on a project entitled, 'Eastern Partnership Countries on the cross-roads of the Eurasian Geopolitics: USA, EU, Russia, and China'. His research and teaching cover international relations, geopolitics, as well as international and cyber security, with focus on the South Caucasus, Eastern Europe, Russia, and Eurasia.

Diana Galoyan serves as the Rector of the Armenian State University of Economics, holding a Doctor of Economics degree and the title of Professor. During her tenure at the university, she has held various roles, including professorships, vice-rectorships, and leadership positions within departments. Dr Galoyan has also taught at various leading European and Russian universities and has been a guest lecturer at numerous prominent European universities. Her publications cover a wide range of topics, including the transmission mechanisms of economic shocks within the Eurasian Economic Union, the impact of the COVID-19 pandemic on mortality rates, and assessments of capital flows among regional economic associations. Galoyan's research orientation also encompasses issues such as EU politics, policies and polity and interregional differences in quality of life and the development of youth entrepreneurship.

Albert Hayrapetyan, PhD in Economics, serves as a Senior Lecturer in the Department of International Economic Relations at the Armenian State University of Economics. He is a CERGE-EI Teaching Fellow. Dr. Hayrapetyan's areas of expertise include EU politics, policies, and regional integration. He has earned Master's degrees from the College of Europe and the American University of Armenia. Dr. Hayrapetyan is the author of numerous scientific articles and four collaborative monographs. Notably, he translated Prince Hans-Adam II of Liechtenstein's 'The State in the Third Millennium' into Armenian. He is credited as one of the first Armenian scholars to publish a comprehensive legal study on Nagorno-Karabakh. Dr. Hayrapetyan has guest lectured at the University of Applied Sciences BFI Vienna, the University of Gdansk, Poznan University of Economics and Business, and Corvinus University of Budapest.

Nino Jibuti is a Tbilisi-based Project Manager with more than 10 years of experience in development projects in various fields. Her thematic areas of interest are good governance, civil activism, conflict resolution, South Caucasus, rural development policy, and empowerment of vulnerable groups. Nino served as a research fellow at the Eastern Partnership Civil Society Fellowship Program where her research explored the connection between Youth Internal Migration and Youth Civic activism in Georgia.

Nino has vast experience in implementing different foreign donor-supported programs at local and international organizations such as the Georgian Institute of Politics (GIP), American Councils, Georgian Farmers Association (GFA), etc. Nino earned an undergraduate degree in Social and Political Science Faculty at Ivane Javakhishvili State University (TSU), during which she spent an academic year at Charles University in Prague, Czechia, on a bilateral exchange scholarship program. Nino received her European Master's Degree in Social Policy through a joint program comprising of consortium of universities ISCTE—Lisbon, Portugal, University of Stavanger—Stavanger, Norway, and Gothenburg University in Gothenburg, Sweden.

Thomas Kruessmann is a professor of criminal law at the Institute of European and Comparative Criminal Law of New Vision University Tbilisi (Georgia) As President of the Association of European Studies for the Caucasus, he devotes himself to European Studies in the wider Caucasus region. He is a German-qualified lawyer with extensive legal practice in one of Vienna's leading law firms. He is also founding director of the Russian, East European & Eurasian Studies Centre at the University of Graz (2010-2015) and Visiting Professor at Kazan Federal University (2015-16). Beyond the Caucasus, his research interests extend to issues of comparative, European and international criminal law, gender and the law as well as corruption and compliance.

Ivanna Machitidze obtained her MA degree in International Relations and European Studies from Central European University (Austria/Hungary) and the PhD degree from Donetsk National University (Ukraine) with specialization in Comparative Political Systems.

Ivanna is the Assoc. Prof. of International Relations at the Faculty of Social Sciences, Education and Humanities at the International Black Sea University. Since January 2019 Dr. Machitidze has been the Accreditation Expert of educational programs in the field of Political Science and International Relations. Her research interests include regionalism and democratization-related issues with a focus on the Black Sea area, in particular Ukraine and the South Caucasus.

Archil Sikharulidze is founder of the Tbilisi-based research institute SIKHA foundation that focuses on academic research, analysis in political and social sciences; additionally, implementation of the modern technologies to the higher education system of Georgia. Mr. Sikharulidze is a senior researcher/scholar and a software developer. He holds master's degrees in Public Administration (MPA) from the Robert Gordon University (RGU) and in International Relations (MA) from the Ivane Javakhishvili Tbilisi State University (TSU). His research areas are Russian & Islamic Studies, Ukraine, South Caucasus and Kazakhstan. Mr. Sikharulidze has written the monography 'Russia 1991 – 2008' which is widely acknowledged in Georgia.

ibidem*.eu*